Urban Economics

Harry W. Richardson

Penguin Books

Penguin Books Ltd, Harmondsworth,
Middlesex, England
Penguin Books Inc., 7110 Ambassador Road,
Baltimore, Md 21207, U.S.A.
Penguin Books Australia Ltd,
Ringwood, Victoria, Australia

First published 1971
Copyright © Harry W. Richardson, 1971

Made and printed in Great Britain by
Richard Clay (The Chaucer Press) Ltd,
Bungay, Suffolk
Set in Monotype Times

Penguin Modern Economics Texts

This volume is one in a series of unit texts designed to reduce the price of knowledge for students of economics in universities and colleges of higher education. The units may be used singly or in combination with other units to form attractive and unusual teaching programmes. The volumes will cover the major teaching areas but they will differ from conventional books in their attempt to chart and explore new directions in economic thinking. The traditional divisions of theory and applied, of positive and normative and of micro and macro will tend to be blurred as authors impose new and arresting ideas on the traditional corpus of economics. Some units will fall into conventional patterns of thought but many will transgress established beliefs.

Penguin Modern Economic Texts are published in units in order to achieve certain objectives. First, a large range of short texts at inexpensive prices gives the teacher flexibility in planning his course and recommending texts for it. Secondly, the pace at which important new work is published requires the project to be adaptable. Our plan allows a unit to be revised or a fresh unit to be added with maximum speed and minimal cost to the reader.

The international range of authorship will, it is hoped, bring out the richness and diversity in economic analysis and thinking.

B. J. MCC.

Penguin Education

Penguin Modern Economics Texts
General Editor: B. J. McCormick

Political Economy
Editor: K. J. W. Alexander

Urban Economics
Harry W. Richardson

Contents

Editorial Foreword

It is a particular pleasure to write an Editorial Foreword to this book as it so successfully fulfils one of the aims of the series: the exploration of one of the areas of economics which though of major importance is seriously under-provided for in text-book form. Harry Richardson's earlier text in this series has been recognized as meeting an important contribution to the understanding and teaching of regional economics. This text is complementary to the earlier volume, drawing upon many of the same theoretical concepts and applying them and others in a more specialized area. The area is one of special difficulty for economic analysis for reasons which the author outlines. Because of this it is important not only that the student should be introduced to the relevant theories and techniques and shown how they may be applied, but that their limitations should be very carefully stressed and the scope for judgement given due weight. This difficult balance is most effectively struck within the confines of a short text. I am confident that it will be of great value to students of economics and of planning, and to the growing band of those concerned with decision-taking affecting the future shape and texture of city life.

K.J.W.A.

Preface

This book may be regarded as a companion volume to my earlier text in this series on regional economics. Whereas *Elements of Regional Economics* dealt with the broader aspects of space such as the links between regions and urban-regional relationships, this book concentrates on economic problems arising within the single city. This focus is easily justified by the importance of the subject, since it could be argued that the problems of how to allocate urban resources efficiently and to maintain the quality of life in our cities are among the most serious questions facing society in the rest of this century. My major concern has been with the principles and theory of urban economics, but another objective has been to include sufficient empirical observations to make the discussion concrete. The context for the analysis is that of cities in highly urbanized, advanced industrial economies, though I hope that the dangers of writing about a fictitious city somewhere in mid-Atlantic have been avoided.

I wish to thank Professor Kenneth Alexander, Murray Stewart and Joan Vipond for their constructive comments. I am very grateful to Mrs Sandy Sharples for typing the drafts.

Introduction:
Economics and Urban Problems

Of all the challenges and problems that face mankind in the rest of the century there are few that look so intractable yet affect so closely the daily lives of so many people as the problem of the city. It is true of course that the majority of the world's population still lives in the country, but the proportion of city dwellers increases rapidly year by year. Yet economics, which as a discipline has done so much towards solving poverty and unemployment, underdevelopment, the population explosion, and other problems, has not given a great deal of attention to the city. Despite the surge of interest in urban economics in the last decade, especially in the United States, urban economists are still thin on the ground. The few there are frequently have to endure the condescension of their purist colleagues because they are not concerned with the great traditional themes and because they fraternize with sociologists, planners and similar types. But surely it would be a sad comment on the state of economics if it had nothing to offer to aid our understanding of urban problems. This is underlined if we subscribe to the view sometimes propounded (even by economists) that in many branches of the subject, research is already showing diminishing returns. No one could maintain this position in regard to urban economics. It is not simply that urban economics raises some unsettled questions, but rather that *none* of the problems have been solved.

One of the major explanations of why economists have been reluctant to analyse the city is that the city does not yield its secrets to conventional economic analysis. There are many reasons why this is so. One of the most important is that the city is riddled with externalities, and as is well known the presence of externalities makes it difficult, if not impossible, to allocate resources optimally. Another factor is that so many urban investments are 'lumpy'. Obviously, economies and diseconomies of scale are strongly associated with this discontinuity in investment decisions. Although the lumpiness and the scale economies are easier to handle with available tools of economic analysis than externalities, the absence of a constant returns to scale assumption makes neoclassical marginalism inapplicable. A further point on similar lines is the absence of a market for many urban goods and services. Public investment predominates in urban infrastructure, and so many of the services supplied by the public sector never appear on the market. It is impossible to define the need for a particular public good. Preferences can only be revealed very imperfectly through political mechanisms. As Harris (1965) has suggested, one attempted solution is to create a pseudo-market with the aid of either cost-benefit analysis or user charges. Even so, economic analysis does not provide a clear-cut answer as to how resources should be allocated between public and private investments in urban communities.

Even where market forces are important in cities, the market is far from perfect. First, many actors on the urban scene exercise a degree of monopoly power particularly in the urban land market: prominent amongst these actors are the planning authority itself, property companies, mortgage institutions, sellers of land, builders and the design professions. Secondly, externalities ensure that the market does not bring about an optimal use of land, and misallocation shows itself as central city congestion and urban sprawl. Most significant of all, the urban land market is characterized by severe rigidities. Establishments have a very strong preference for their existing sites. The main reason for this is that investment in site improvement has a long life, is costly and, because of the specificity of individual establishments, is not easily recoverable on the market. If the city is growing, the allocation of a given activity to a given site is likely to remain optimal only for a short time, yet resources are not easily transferred once they have been committed. The costs of changing sites can be very high: losses are possible on the initial investment; seeking a new location can be time-consuming and expensive; property transaction costs are high. These rigidities cannot easily be coped with by using conventional economic analysis.

One of the most serious of all the obstacles restricting the application of economic analysis is the immense complexity of urban life. The normal procedure in economic theory is to represent a 'stylized facts' version of reality by constructing a model with the aid of a number of simplifying assumptions and by keeping down the number of variables to manageable proportions. It is then customary to proceed on *ceteris paribus* lines, and this usually means the employment of partial equilibrium models.[1] It is difficult when analysing the city to achieve anything very constructive with models of this kind. For instance, the interaction between public investment and land use decisions and the actions of private households and firms in the market, and the feedback of one upon the other, are not easily taken into account in a partial equilibrium approach. In addition, the urban economy must, if it is to be understood, be conceived of in terms of more dimensions than is customary in most branches of economic analysis. We cannot comprehend it with static resource allocation models that determine the optimal combination of factors in a spaceless, timeless world.[2] The city, if it is anything, is a dynamic phenomenon with real spatial coordinates. It grows not only over time but in space; indeed, it grows upwards (in density) as well as outwards (in area) yet there is no satisfactory model of urban growth to accommodate both types of increase. We can, of course, use partial models to determine, say, the

1. Over the years economists have made some, even impressive, headway in general equilibrium theory, but the models in this field are usually grossly oversimplified. See Kuenne (1963).

2. What can we say about urban location for instance if we abstract from time and space, especially if we accept Blumenfeld's dictum (1964), that 'everyone who makes a decision on location of residence or of business is engaged in a trade-off between minimizing time or maximizing space'?

optimal location for a retail firm provided we make some very restrictive assumptions about the spatial structure of the city and freeze it in space and time. But while they are useful for certain purposes (and I cannot avoid making use of this kind of model elsewhere in this book), they do not tell us what makes the city work. For within the city everything seems related to everything else, and perhaps the chief characteristic of the urban economy is its interdependence. The economist armed with his kit of familiar tools is likely to be confused and bewildered when asked to dissect the city. As Hoover has put it:

Picturing all this even in greatly simplified terms as an equilibrium or dynamic system, the model builder or other theoretician, trying to encompass the whole, is likely to find himself hopelessly engulfed in myriad simultaneous equations, in futile search of a useful solution or any solution (1968, p. 237).

Yet such pessimism cannot be used as an excuse for abdication of responsibility by the economist. For as the editors of the book in which the above quotation appears state:

The analysis and evaluation of the economies of urban scale, the role of the CBD in the economic health of the metropolitan region, the role of the urban slum in the exacerbation or perpetuation of poverty, the interdependence of land and capital markets with urban development policies – these and similar areas of economic ignorance are now ready for the economist's unique techniques of analysis, his capacity for specification and, most important of all, his special insights into the allocative processes of society (Perloff and Wingo, 1968).

1 Location

Introduction

Analysis of the location of particular types of activity and the spatial structure of the city as a whole must begin from three general factors of importance in the urban economy: market mechanisms and the constraints under which they operate; external and other agglomeration economies; and transport costs.

The market is important because the spatial organization of the city is largely the result of a process that allocates activities to sites, and this process is derived to a great extent from free contracts between suppliers of and purchasers (or tenants) of urban land. Market mechanisms underlie even those urban phenomena that might appear to be primarily social in origin and character – slums, central area blight, suburban sprawl. But competition in the urban land market is not unconstrained. Inertia and high mobility costs prevent a high proportion of urban land that is in sub-optimal use from coming on to the market. The market is even more distorted by compulsory purchase, zoning and other land use constraints, and by property tax (or rating) policies. Similarly, a substantial proportion of centrally located urban land is swallowed up by public investments; roads are the dominant example. Even so, these distortions do not erode the central feature of the urban land market: that the price (rent) of land is an inverse function (typically a negative exponential function) of distance from the city centre.

This rent/distance function primarily reflects the influence of two major factors: external and other agglomeration economies and transport costs.[1] The significance of transport costs is obvious. People and activities are drawn into cities because of a need for mutual accessibility, especially between homes and workplaces. Even within cities, the distances between interrelated activities have to be minimized, and the existence of transport costs tends *ceteris paribus* to draw activities together.

The role of external economies, neighbourhood effects and agglomeration economies generally is less obvious but probably more significant. Tsuru (1963) has argued that 'the economic significance of cities lies in the external economies they provide', while Lampard (1963) has suggested that urban growth is the spatial manifestation of increasing returns to scale and external economies. Agglomeration economies would probably induce activities to cluster together spatially even in the absence of transport costs or high land prices. They include: scale economies at the firm or industry level, external economies including access to a common labour market, benefits gained from personal contacts and the provision of business services, access to population and market potential, environmental factors and neighbourhood effects. With regard to the latter, as a generalization, an activity benefits from locating near to similar factors, for example the clustering of high income households. In addition, there are certain urban facilities that can only be supported by a high threshold population level. These may include leisure and cultural amenities such as an orchestra or theatre, or transport and public service facilities such as a jet airport, a specialist hospital or a computer complex servicing local business.

It is easy enough to give a long list of agglomeration and external economies. The problem arises when we attempt to

1. It is perhaps significant that Blumenfeld (1964) defines the metropolis in terms of scale and transport costs as an area containing in excess of half a million population living at a distance of less than forty-five minutes travel time from its centre by modes available to the majority of the population. For further discussion of the role of agglomeration economies, and transport costs in location decisions (see Richardson, 1969b, pp. 70–78).

quantify their impact. It is probable that the character of urban growth and the size distribution of urban centres are determined largely by the balance of external economies and diseconomies, yet so great is our ignorance that it is unclear whether urban concentration confers net social costs or benefits, or, if the answer to this depends on the size of the concentrations, where exactly the optimal point occurs. Baumol (1967) implies that cities have already reached or exceeded their optimal size by suggesting that external diseconomies are increasing faster than population. Of more general importance is that Baumol's hypothesis of a functional relationship between external diseconomies and population could also apply to external economies. The more general hypothesis is that external economies (or diseconomies) of an urban area are a function of the square of the number of its inhabitants:

$$E = aP^2,$$

where E equals the external economies, and P is the population. The rationale of this hypothesis is as follows. If each inhabitant in an area imposes external costs (or benefits) on every other, and if the size of the costs borne (or benefits gained) by each individual is roughly proportional to population size (or density) then, since these costs (benefits) apply to each of the n persons involved, the total external costs (benefits) will vary not in proportion to n but to n^2. I have argued elsewhere (Richardson, 1969b, p. 100) on similar lines that the influence of external economies and diseconomies might be quantified by applying exponents to scale variables, particularly in gravity models. Where I differ from the above analysis is in believing that the exponent will normally be less than 2 though greater than 1, and that its value will not remain constant with changes in population size. Instead, the exponent will change in value as n increases. Only in this way is it possible to retain a function relating external economies and diseconomies to urban population, and yet account for the transition from net economies to net diseconomies at a particular city size. It would be a useful starting-point for testing these hypotheses to see how relevant measures (for example the *per capita* cost of urban services, traffic congestion or productivity of retail and business firms) varies with urban population levels.

These general considerations should be kept in mind not only in this chapter on location and in the next on spatial structure, but as relevant to many of the issues raised in the rest of the book – growth, transport, renewal, fiscal problems and planning.

Residential location decisions

The importance of residential location decisions can hardly be challenged. Housing is by far the largest use to which urban land is put (perhaps about one-half of the total). Consequently, as the total amount of land within an area is essentially fixed apart from outward shifts in the boundary, the spatial distribution of residences in an urban area has profound implications for the structure of urban land values. Moreover, households may spend up to 25 per cent of their disposable income on housing. An analysis of the determinants of residential location therefore needs no apology.

Some writers have looked at the problem of household location from the viewpoint of macrospatial structure, and have developed models which describe the aggregate spatial pattern of distribution of residences over the whole urban area (Herbert and Stevens, 1961; Lowry,1 964; Chapin, 1965b; Arthur D. Little Inc., 1966a; Swerdloff and Stowers, 1966; Wilson, 1968). The alternative, what we may call the microeconomic, approach is to concentrate on the individual household and to explain its location decision in terms of its choices and preferences. Although they are difficult to make operational, behavioural models of this type have the considerable advantage of focusing on the actions of individual decision-makers.

Of the behavioural models of household location (if we count all the subtle variants there are a great many), there are two groups which have received and merit special attention.

The first type makes journey to work costs (whether measured in money and/or time) the main explanatory variable. In extreme versions, this means explaining residential location decisions in terms of minimising travel costs; in more moderate and more acceptable forms, the models emphasise the importance of trade-offs between travel costs and housing costs (location rent) – what Hoover (1968) calls the 'access/ space trade-off'. Models of this kind have been developed by Schnore (1965), Kain (1962), Wingo (1961) and Alonso (1964). The second major alternative approach consists of theories which stress choice of house and area and environmental preferences as the principal determinants of residential location; the role of journey to work costs/time is relegated to that of an outer constraint. This line of thought is found in the work of, among others, Ellis (1967) and Stegman (1969). My preference is for the latter approach on the ground that trade-off hypotheses seem inconsistent with how households actually behave. In consequence, I wish to outline a theory of household location which stresses environmental preferences but also has its own special features not incorporated in other theories.

A critique of trade-off models

The popularity of trade-off models makes it necessary to subject them to some scrutiny. The extreme travel cost minimization hypothesis need not detain us very long. According to this hypothesis, households should live as close to the workplace as possible. This is completely inconsistent with empirical observation. If the hypothesis were valid, the rich (with more purchasing power available and therefore the ability to outbid lower income groups for any site) would live near the city centre, whereas higher income groups tend to live on the outskirts. Secondly, a great deal of evidence in the United States (Lansing and Mueller, 1964; Lansing, 1966; Lapin, 1964; Loewenstein, 1965; Stegman, 1969) shows that changes of residences are usually associated with a longer, or at least equal, journey to work, and surveys of consumer preferences indicate a strong desire of most households to live further out, if and when they moved. Thirdly, the centrifugal spread of cities is only compatible with travel cost-minimization if jobs are decentralizing as fast as households move into the suburbs. To the extent that journey-to-work minimization predicts locational behaviour this applies only to the very poor and the very rich. The poor have to live near work because they cannot afford the fares, while the very rich may live centrally on high cost land because of the high valuation they put on their time.

Trade-off hypotheses are much more difficult to dispose of. It is usually assumed that: households substitute travel costs for housing costs and the rate of substitution is governed by each household's preference for high or low density living; jobs are centralized; travel costs are a steadily increasing function of distance, while site rents (or price per unit of land) decline with distance; rising incomes will normally tend to be associated with a propensity to consume more space.

Following Wingo (1961), we may assume that a household in a given income class as a constant sum to spend on housing and transport costs after meeting all other expenditure demands on its income, Y_{h+t}. The household can choose who it wishes to allocate this sum between housing costs and travel. If the household chooses a site at m and the city centre is represented by o we may write

$$Y_{h+t} = p_m q_m + t_{om} \tag{1}$$

where p and q represent the price and quantity of land (and housing) consumed and t equals transport costs.

Rearranging,

$$p_m q_m = Y_{h+t} - t_{om} \tag{2}$$

Thus expenditure on housing is a function of transport cost savings. The demand curve for land is downward sloping, i.e. the lower the price of land the more will be consumed, and this can be expressed as

$$q_m = \left[\frac{a}{p_m} \right]^b \tag{3}$$

where a and b are parametric constants and $b > 0$. Where the household will locate depends on its income, its preferences for residential space and the unit price of residential space. Taking the workplace and transport costs as given, the household's location can be expressed as a function of its space consumption. Abstracting from changes in mode or the existence of different classes of travel, transport costs will be the same for all households regardless of their income. The rich will consequently have more to spend on housing; they can choose between greater access (higher p, but lower t and q) and more space (lower p, but higher t and q). As stated above, the normal assumption is that the income elasticity of demand for space is positive. Thus, the richer will tend to live further out and at lower residential densities than those on lower incomes, and are content to put up with a longer journey to work.

Harris (1968) has argued that this tendency for the wealthy to live on the outskirts could be explained by factors other than optimizing between increased space and shorter work trips. For example, the housing preferences of the wealthy may relate to good housing conditions and neighbourhood cleanliness rather than to low density, and these characteristics may be found only in the low density suburban areas; or suburban living might be explained by a desire of high income groups to segregate themselves from the poor (in Britain) or from Negroes (in the United States). Muth (1968a) has suggested that the tendency for average incomes to increase with distance is largely due to the intercorrelation of both variables with the age of the dwelling in question. In other words, people prefer new houses and these are found on the outskirts of cities. Consequently and not surprisingly, that is where those who can afford to satisfy their preferences live. Stegman (1969) stresses the importance of improved quality of housing, amenity and environmental conditions rather than more residential space as reasons why households are willing to sacrifice proximity to the city centre. He also points out that land of the inner core is dominated by non-residential uses which can normally outbid residential users; consequently, more land suitable for housing can be purchased farther out at lower prices. Most radical of all his arguments, however, is that the decentralization of work and shopping activities and the construction of fast roads is making urban services and activities more accessible to suburban than to central city households. As yet, this development is more prevalent in the United States than in Britain. However, in cases where it is true the result is that 'large numbers of suburban families do not have to trade off accessibility for savings in location rent; they can have both' (Stegman, p. 22). His arguments also imply that accessibility to a wide range of activities and journeys, other than to work, are having a relatively greater influence on household location decisions.

Despite these empirical objections, there is no doubt that the trade-off thesis is attractive with its emphasis on a household's rational calculations of a choice between more space and/or cheaper housing on the one hand, and shorter journeys to work and greater accessibility on the other. Moreover, the two crucial assumptions for the hypothesis – that costs of site occupancy decline and that transport costs increase with distance – accord with casual empirical observation in large cities. The aggregate inverse relationship between house prices and travel costs is much less clear. Around London, for example, high class, expensive and low density housing is not found solely on the outer boundaries of the commuting area nor does it occur concentrically. Rather it is heavily concentrated in a broad and deep band to the west (south-west) in Surrey and the Chilterns. House prices can vary enormously within a small geographical area owing to differences in site amenity, variations in structure and type, quality of fittings, differences in builders' pricing policies and short-run supply and demand conditions. Local rent peaks are found at developed centres some distance from London breaking up the smoothness of the location rent gradient.[2] The site value of a particular location may be

2. Of course, the existence of local rent peaks may be quite compatible with aggregate trade-offs in that they could be explained by the growth of local jobs in the Outer Metropolitan Area centres, which permit

affected substantially by its opportunity cost which may in turn be affected by land use controls and other planning decisions. For these and other reasons, the further assumption that the household trades travel costs for more *space* is critical for the trade-off models to work, since densities in a given price range undoubtedly fall with distance. Most trade-off theorists do in fact make this additional assumption.

Even if there is a marked inverse relationship between site costs and travel costs, this does not necessarily support trade-off behaviour by households. It may be what is called an aggregate *derived* relationship which can only be properly tested with microeconomic data.[3] Furthermore, another objection to a facile switch from aggregate to micro-relationships is that the location decisions of households are distributed over time, and in long-established settlements the link between the individual decision and the overall relationship will be weak and tenuous, except in the special case when location rents and transport costs have always changed at the same rate. Individual households do not move in response to variations in housing or travel costs except when other factors intervene, e.g. a change of job, a newly formed household, or a change in family size requiring a larger or smaller house.

The trade-off models become considerably weaker once the assumption of centralized employment opportunities is dropped. Jobs are becoming increasingly decentralized, while in very prosperous regions such as south-east England intervening opportunities must not be neglected. Individuals are often happy to travel longer distances to work in order to get a better paid and more satisfying job.

A final, and by no means the least damaging, drawback to trade-off hypotheses is that they assume complete freedom of

employees to reduce their travel costs by not having to commute to London. Because their travel costs are lower, they are willing to pay more for housing.

3. For an explanation of this argument see Duesenberry's article, especially pp. 62–5, reprinted in Mueller (1966).

choice and near perfect competition. For instance, they assume elasticity in the short-run supply of housing and no mono-polistic elements in the housing market, neither of which is tenable. Trade-off requires that a household can choose a location anywhere between the city centre and the outer boundary of the commuting zone (subject to an income constraint). But given that in many cases the household has to choose a house within a fairly short space of time, and that the supply of houses within the potential range of locations may be severely restricted, the freedom of choice may be limited. There may be only a very small number of houses which can satisfy the household's requirements; in many cases, these could all be in a similar price range yet be varied enough in location to imply very different journey-to-work lengths. Furthermore, the models imply the existence of a trade-off curve between housing costs and journey-to-work costs on which the household can pay for housing any sum (monthly mortgage repayment or rent) between the minimum and the maximum housing cost points on the curve. This is very rarely possible. The range of monthly housing costs may be severely constrained by the amount of mortgage finance the household can obtain. The trade-off curve may degenerate into a small segment near the minimum housing cost point, or even to a single point. The household may thus be faced with the narrow choice of locating at a great distance from work in order to get cheap housing of a type it prefers or accepting a cramped, substandard house near work.

The elements of a new model

The behavioural theory of residential location developed here places great emphasis on owner-occupiers. The argument is that for such groups housing preferences (including the kind of area and quality of environment that the household desires) and financial constraints, that is income and the conditions and availability of mortgage finance, are the primary independent variables, and that journey to work costs are at best a secondary determinant and in many cases are determined residually with no explanatory significance whatsoever. Of course, the journey to work must act as a constraint in that there is a maximum commuting limit in travel time, and there is probably also a maximum journey-to-work cost for each income class.

For most income groups the residential location decision is constrained by the ability to get a mortgage. Households generally tend to select a house as expensive as they can afford,[4] so that residential location decisions can be interpreted in terms of households' *maximizing housing costs*, subject to the constraints of their income and the willingness of building societies and other mortgage agencies to make advances to them. Having determined the price range they can afford, households then look around at houses within this range which satisfy certain predetermined requirements (for example the type of house, the number of bedrooms, the existence of garage and garden, a preferred area, etc.). The area of search may be quite large, and will vary in size according to the available stock of houses on the market, personal preferences based on casual observation of localities, areas in which work colleagues live, areas containing or with access to good schools, etc. This area will also vary between households according to their flexibility, knowledge of the region, point of origin of the house search and the houses available near it, and many other factors. In most cases, journey to work costs will not have much of an influence provided that the area of search falls within commuting limits. Of course, if the household lacks a car, access to public transport facilities will exert an influence, but for single car-owning households desiring a semi-rural or rural location, other journeys (to school, or to shops for example) may be more influential than the journey to work. In other words, within their ability-to-pay constraint households maximise their utility gain by choosing the house which most closely meets their requirements in a location

4. One reason for this in Britain is the fact that tax relief on the interest component of mortgage repayments makes the annual cost of a house much lower than its annual rate of capital appreciation.

which matches as far as possible their area and local site preferences. At best, journey to work costs will be one of many factors compounded in this decision; in the vast majority of cases the location decision will be ultimately determined by choice of a particular house rather than by choice of location near work.

If owner-occupiers maximize housing costs, if building societies pay no attention in determining the mortgage advance to other claims on household expenditure, and if cheaper houses are found on the periphery of cities, then low income households may find themselves in a situation where they have to pay high journey-to-work costs relative to their income. There are very large numbers of these households in the Outer Metropolitan Area around London, and their presence there conflicts with the trade-off hypothesis.

Another point is that households choosing to locate at the periphery do not invariably choose low-density dwellings. Indeed, many households locate near the outer limits in residences with densities similar to those much more centrally situated. This strengthens the argument that households locate peripherally, not to offset high travel costs by location rents which are low enough to enable them to satisfy greater space preferences (Kain, 1962), but simply because they prefer to live there, thus supporting a general area preference hypothesis. Moreover, in south-east England, where property values are high in accessible pleasant areas, the medium to upper income groups are found both near London and at great distances from it. This contradicts the travel cost minimization approach, and can be explained most easily by the fact that tastes are heterogeneous. These households are probably maximizing their housing costs *and* expressing area preferences; that some of the locations involve a much shorter journey to work may be irrelevant.

A theory of residential location of this kind may be expressed more formally as follows. The amount of money a household will spend on a house will tend towards a maximum $a_t Y_t$ where a_t is the maximum mortgage/income ratio that the finance agency is willing to lend to households of income class i, and Y_i equals the income of household i.

We may write

$$H_i = p_m q_m, \tag{4}$$

where $H_i(a_i Y_i)$ is the price of the selected house, p_m equals the unit price of housing at location m and q_m is the quantity of housing purchased at m, which is a weighted average of size of site and size of house required. The unit price of land is a direct function of the quality of the environment and amenity of the area, n, and an inverse function of distance from the city centre. If we adopt the familiar negative exponential distance function concept we may write

$$p_m = Jn_m e^{-Kd_{om}}, \tag{5}$$

where n_m is an index of environment/quality of area at location m, e is the usual Naperian logarithm, d_{om} is the distance between the city centre o and location m, and J and K are constants. According to this model housing preferences will be determined by the household's area/environmental and size of site/house requirements; in other words, the housing preference function takes the form

$$D_{H_i} = f(n_i, q_i).$$

(It is probable that q_i will in turn be dependent upon the household's family size, stage of family cycle and income, but this can be ignored for simplification.) Given the housing preference function, $f(n_i, q_i)$, the household will locate at that site which most satisfactorily meet its environmental and size preferences and which satisfies the equation

$$a_i Y_i = Jn_m e^{-Kd_{om}} q_m, \tag{6}$$

(obtained by substituting $a_i Y_i$ for H_i and by substituting 5 into 4) subject to the constraint

$$d_{om} \leqslant d_x,$$

where d_x equals maximum commuting distance. Thus, in this model d_{om} is determined residually.

The implications for planning of how households decide where to live cannot be overemphasized, especially in an age characterized by increasing job mobility and growing overspill problems. In a situation where jobs cannot be decentralized fast enough, then the appropriate prescription for transportation planning from travel-cost minimisation models is to improve speeds and reduce costs, and for the planning of housing to build at very high densities as centrally as possible. On the other hand, if households locate primarily to satisfy housing preferences, then more emphasis should be given to supplying the type of houses people want in the kind of environment and area they desire; this might be more important than marginal reductions in travel time. These are only illustrative possibilities. The general point is that knowing why people choose to live at particular locations and understanding the role played by the journey to work in these decisions is of fundamental importance to planners, helping them to answer such questions as: How far is it necessary to encourage decentralization of employment? What types of housing should be built and where? How should the allocation of investment priorities between, say, improving suburban environments and making the transportation network to the central city more efficient be determined? Can peripheral regional growth points compete with large metropolises, and what types of investment (for example in local transport networks, or in housing and general amenities) are necessary to improve their competitiveness?

Non-residential establishments
Introduction

It is virtually impossible to devise a comprehensive theory of non-residential location, either for non-residential establishments as a whole or for particular types (shops, offices, factories, etc.). The concept of an optimal location is difficult to introduce into an established city since the best sites may already have been pre-empted and there is such inertia and stability in the occupation of urban sites that sub-optimality is the general rule. Furthermore, optimizing models are usually static. An explanation of urban location in static terms is, to say the least, incomplete, since the dynamics of urban change can drastically affect the relative value of the key locational determinants. Such factors include changes in the level and spatial distribution of population, transport improvements, technological change in production and (especially) communications, pressure for central area redevelopment and many more. The mass of evidence on suburbanization (decentralization) of population, industry and services, suggests that the optimal location may have changed for many activities, but this evidence is difficult to interpret since decentralization trends vary in strength from city to city, between countries and over time.[5] The analysis would be easier if particular functions were to confine selected sites to certain parts of the city; for instance if offices, banks and department stores were to occupy the central core with warehousing, wholesaling and light manufacturing an inner ring, residences an outer ring, manufacturing located on the periphery of the city, and agriculture further out still in rural areas. But a neat concentric zone structure of this kind is not supported by reality. In fact, identical types of establishment often thrive in the CBD (central business district), in the suburbs and in small towns. As a generalization, within an urban area there is unlikely to be a unique optimal location. Irregularities in the scope of the rent gradient and curvilinearity in the variation of other costs and revenues with distance from the city centre suggest that there may be more than one equally good site for each establishment within the city.

For all these reasons, any attempt to construct a general theory of urban location is bound to be unsatisfactory. Typical of the best of such attempts is Alonso's theory which derives from von Thünen's work on agricultural location and

5. How to pinpoint in time the beginnings of the suburbanization trend is complex, and the views of urban analysts are often conflicting. For a recent study of the United States, see Mills (1969).

also owes a debt to Haig's analysis in the 1920s.[6] The essence of the Alonso model is that activities can offset declining revenue and higher operating (including transport) costs by lower site rents at locations increasingly distant from the city centre. There will be some rent (called the *bid rent*) which an activity will be prepared to pay at each site, when this bid rent is defined as the rent which would allow the firm to maintain the same profit level (that is would exactly compensate for falling revenue and higher costs). The equilibrium location for a firm is when its bid rent equals the actual rent ruling at a site (on the assumption that the structure of land prices is given, and that rents vary inversely with distance). For each activity a family of bid rent functions can be derived, and the activities with the steeper bid rent curves capture the central locations because they are prepared to pay more for central sites. 'Preparedness to pay' reflects the activity's need for a central location. Indeed, with profits held constant, the rate of change of the total bid rent for an activity is equal to the rate of change in the volume of business minus the rate of change in operating costs.

The Alonso model rests on simplified assumptions: a centralized city with a single nucleus, a perfect market for urban land, agglomerating forces and locational interdependence are ignored as are special site characteristics and topographical irregularities. However, these qualifications can easily be taken into account. More serious is what we lose as a consequence of the gain in generality. The Alonso model allocates activities $i, j, k, l, \ldots, n$ to sites according to the steepness of their bid rent curves, but offers no guidance as to what these activities might be. The heterogeneity of non-residential activities suggests that we may need the location of offices, shops, manufacturing plants and other establishments to be explained separately.

6. See Haig (1926). The brevity with which Alonso's theory is dealt here is not an indication of its importance. However, his work is easily accessible (see Alonso, 1960, 1964). For a summary see Richardson (1969a, pp. 129–32).

Revenue and cost gradients

An obvious approach to urban location is to explore how total costs and revenues vary over the area of the city. This is much more difficult than appears at first sight, however. Space cost curves will vary widely from one firm to another, because cost-distance functions for different items of cost (land, wages, capital, transport) may follow separate paths, and because firms even in the same sector will consume different inputs in different amounts. A single-storey factory with heavy space demands will have a cost structure grossly dissimilar to that of, say, a factory for making scientific instruments. Moreover, since the input structure can alter with changes in scale, costs will vary even among firms in the same industry (Alonso, 1967). If costs vary with scale of output, then it cannot be assumed that the total cost curve and the total revenue curve for a particular establishment are independent. And if revenue is also in many sectors a function of location, analysis of the urban location problem can sink into a morass of interdependencies. Whether revenue varies with distance or not depends very much on the type of activity involved. A department store or a business equipment sales establishment may be able to thrive only in the central core, but for a manufacturing firm catering for non-local markets revenue can be assumed constant regardless of whereabouts in or near the city it is located.

Given these difficulties, and in the context of the present discussion which is concerned with general principles rather than the locational determinants of an individual firm in a single industry, it is wise to restrict comment to broad statements about revenue and cost gradients.[7]

Revenue. For certain activities, especially retail trade, population is an approximate measure of market potential. In

7. The virtue of the Alonso model is that all the variations in cost and revenue with distance are subsumed in the bid rent function. However, although this simplifies the theory it does not make it any easier to apply, since the bid rent function can be derived only by knowing how individual items of cost and revenue vary, or by revealed preference.

modern cities, the resident population gradient tends to decline with increasing distance from the city centre, except that the curve 'caves in' in the CBD itself, reflecting the expulsion of dwellings from the central core as the pressure for high value central sites has increased. But the resident population gradient is not the best measure of retail market potential even as an approximation. In the first place, the distribution of daytime population is more important, and this may be measured for a given zone by adding the working population in that zone to the residents and deducting the number of residents working outside the zone. Secondly, since people will travel a certain distance to shop, a more precise measure is obtained by an index of population potential. Thirdly, even the daytime population clusters at certain times of the day (for example at lunchtime) so that the points of maximum transit are a more exact indicator of the highest revenue potential. Finally, since buying power is more critical than the number of consumers, the daytime population in any zone needs to be weighted by average income (and by interoccupational differences in the propensity to consume). With all these qualifications, the resulting market potential gradient will be much steeper than the residential population gradient though there will be minor peaks at nuclei located some distance from the CBD.

For business service establishments, the spatial distribution, number and size of client establishments are the main determinants of revenue (and turnover). Since large firms can very often supply themselves with these services, the main market will consist of large numbers of small firms usually sited at central locations. The space revenue curve in these cases will peak sharply in the CBD.

Rent. The price of land will be a negative exponential function of distance, though the gradient need not be smooth. The downward slope of the gradient is the result of acute competition for central sites, and this in turn reflects the demand for accessibility. *Ceteris paribus*, small establishments tend to be able to pay more (in price per square foot) because their space requirements are low and site costs a small proportion of total costs. It can be shown (Wingo, 1961; Moses and Williamson, 1967) that rent must decline with distance for locational equilibrium to hold.

Wages. Whether labour costs vary within the city is an open question. Goldberg (1970a) assumed that they remain constant. But wages may be higher in those parts of the city where employment density is *relatively* higher than residential density, because workers will have to be attracted from a distance and will have to be recompensed for their commuting costs and for the disutility of travelling. Thus, wage levels will normally be higher at the core. On the other hand, if jobs are more decentralised than homes, a suburban firm may have to offer higher wages to switch workers from CBD employment. Although the shape of the wage rate gradient can take many alternative forms according to circumstances, Moses (1962) showed that the wage rate gradient facing a particular firm will slope downwards if the firm's employment is small relative to the population surrounding the potential site.

Capital. Liquid capital is usually assumed perfectly mobile in an urban area and the interest rate is regarded as a locational constant. This is reasonable, though an external economy associated with a core location may be easier access to capital obtained by personal face-to-face contacts with financial institutions, banks and other suppliers of credit.

Transport costs. The influence on transport costs of distance from the core is complex. With a uniform concentric transportation surface and an unrealistic assumption of a fixed distance involved in transporting output and inputs, transport costs will be heavier in the centre due to congestion and will tend to decline with movement away from the core. But these assumptions are restrictive. Other factors are far more important than distance from the centre. These include proximity to suppliers and markets, access to junctions, nodes and terminals, distance between the selected site and the structure of the transport network, and nearness to handling facilities. Generalization is impossible. Desirable locations for manufacturing plants serving outside markets will be found near intercity trunk roads, that is at suburban rather than at central sites. Service establishments with larger labour forces will prefer sites near public transport terminals. It will be much cheaper for department stores to distribute goods to their customers if the stores are centrally located, and obviously such locations are the best for serving personal shoppers. Thus, the better locations from the transportation point of view may vary according to type of activity and will be determined by ease of access to the transport facilities used by the activity. While many of these facilities (for example warehousing and terminal handling facilities) are centrally situated, this is becoming less true over time since even these facilities are being decentralized. The growing reliance on private road transport which is more flexible than rail has reduced the hold of central locations. Transport improvements have widened locational choice, and enabled suburban locations to be substituted for central ones. Moses and Williamson (1967) have gone so far as to argue that the introduction of the truck, first for intraurban transport and later for interregional transport, has been the main force behind the suburbanization of industry. Conversely, the domination of central locations in the late nineteenth century could be explained by the fact that goods were much more costly to move than people, especially at a distance from central goods handling facilities.

Generalizing from the above discussion, factor costs will be lower away from the city core for almost all establishments. Those establishments that still prefer a central location must find that higher costs are offset either by agglomeration economies such as access to complementary firms and specialist services or by higher turnover.

General Principles

Before analysing urban location factors for particular types of establishments, it may simplify matters to list a number of general locational principles. These hold, of course, only on *ceteris paribus* assumptions.

1. Activities serving the city market as a whole are more likely to locate centrally. Activities serving non-local markets will tend to occupy peripheral sites.

2. The more specialized a function, the greater its tendency to occupy a central location.

3. The larger the site area required by an establishment, the more likely it is to acquire a suburban location.[8] This follows from the fact that the price of land tends to be inversely related to distance from the city centre.

4. Urban location decisions are influenced by the existence of land use controls and other urban planning restrictions on the use of central land. If the existence of spatial externalities is accepted (that is that the location decision of one unit has repercussions on the decisions of others[9]), it can be shown that land use controls and zoning have a marked stabilizing effect on the city's location patterns (Tiebout, 1961).

5. The presence of pecuniary external diseconomies (e.g. rising site costs) or technological external diseconomies (smoke, noise, traffic congestion) induces a degree of decentralisation, though the response varies depending on how much an establishment is tied to the central core.

6. The core–suburb dichotomy in urban location decisions needs to be qualified by the fact that large cities usually

8. A qualification here is that in selecting the site for a heavy space-absorbing social facility, for example a sports stadium, the social costs of an off-centre location have to be taken into account. In Amsterdam and Rotterdam, for instance, the peripherally-located stadia create traffic chaos. The site savings may well be outweighed by traffic congestion costs.

9. An obvious example is where a manufacturing firm maximizing its own utility settles in the middle of a residential suburb. This might lead to an endless chain of location moves.

contain secondary centres outside the CBD. In some cases, a site at one of the secondary centres may offer an acceptable compromise.

7. Urban location decisions are interdependent (see (4) above). This interdependence very often shows itself in agglomeration. For instance, agglomeration of similar establishments can create external economies – the ease of face-to-face contacts in the office zone or the fact that locating shops together minimizes commuting costs and attracts custom. Furthermore, complementary activities tend to agglomerate – offices and lunch bars, theatres and restaurants, wholesalers and transport firms. On the other hand, some activities repel each other, for example, nuisance-creating manufactures and high class residences.

8. Historical forces are important in explanations of a city's location pattern. Establishments may continue to occupy central sites long after the *raison d'être* for doing so has passed. Firms do not change their locations immediately it becomes economic to move. A study of Los Angeles (Pegrum, 1963) revealed that industry remained located at the side of the railway even when it no longer made use of it. The age of a city is relevant to understanding the pattern of urban location. In an old city, a high proportion of core sites may be occupied by old-established firms reluctant to move, and even if premises do become free the acquisition and conversion costs of old structures may be high. In a relatively new city, on the other hand, there is greater flexibility of locational choice, good sites available in the suburbs but also less competition for central locations without the problem of too many small plots.

9. The most general of generalizations, based on experience in advanced industrial countries, is that there is increasing locational concentration in a few large cities but a marked decentralization trend within these areas. If this is the case, it suggests that suburban sites on the edge of large cities offer the best of all worlds. They give easy access to the large metropolitan market and to urban amenities and an attractive

environment without having to tolerate the diseconomies, congestion and high costs of central sites.

Location of particular sectors

We have already implied that a general approach to urban location is unsatisfactory because establishments in one sector may have quite different locational requirements from firms in another. Business properties are much more heterogeneous than dwellings. The implications of this fact for location within cities may be illustrated by looking at three sectors: manufacturing, retail trade and office establishments. A more comprehensive survey would bring out this heterogeneity even more.

Manufacturing plants. In nineteenth century cities, manufacturing plants are usually located at central sites. In modern cities, this is no longer true. New plants tend to be established at peripheral sites, for instance in the suburbs or in out-of-town industrial estates, while many old-established firms move, sooner or later, from a core to a decentralized location. The likelihood of outward moves has been increased by transportation improvements and by chances in production methods and factory layout. The substitution of inter-city road freight transport for rail and the development of suburban freight terminals to replace those previously found only in the city centre have given off-centre sites transportation advantages for the carriage of raw materials and finished goods. In many industries the introduction of flow assembly methods has necessitated large-floor-area factories on one storey, and this has made a central location impossible. More generally, many manufacturing firms have found that their cramped core sites have given them too little land on which to extend their plants, while the possibility of acquiring adjacent sites in the centre of the city is very low. Thus, growing firms in growing industries have had a strong incentive to move to a peripheral site with space for expansion. At the same time, there have been several 'push' elements present at core locations: rising site costs for those in leasehold premises; higher rates and property taxes; traffic congestion on the roads. In most cases, these have not been critical factors, but have merely helped to make an outward move more palatable.

For the typical manufacturing firm, then, a suburban location is usually advantageous. Yet many manufacturing firms remain in the central core of cities. There are two major explanations of this. Firstly, many firms remain for non-economic reasons. They have always been in the city centre, they may own their premises, their growth in turnover has probably not given rise to the need for physical extensions, and they see no obvious reason for moving. After all, finding a new site may be tedious and building a new plant costly. It may still be true that if they were to make the necessary calculations the benefits of moving would outweigh the costs, but tradition and inertia rule for the moment.[10]

Secondly, for some manufacturing plants there are still powerful external economies obtainable at the central core and these outweigh higher costs. One of the major economies is labour market accessibility. Especially in cities with a highly developed radial public transport system, labour pool economies are maximized at the city centre. This is particularly important for firms with specialist skilled labour demands. Apart from this, the major characteristic of centrally located manufacturing plants is that they are small scale (Goldberg, 1970a; Vernon, 1960; Cameron and Johnson, 1969). An obvious reason is that small firms have limited space requirements. Many of them may need a central location to service their customers, for example, printing shops with business clients or specialist jewellery manufacturers selling direct to the public.[11] Another important factor is that certain services,

10. When such a firm does relocate, it is usually as a result of 'push' factors, for example because the lease on its premises expires. Moreover, the move is not usually to the best alternative site but merely to an adequate site. See Richardson (1969a, pp. 90–100).

11. A survey of manufacturing firms in Inner London found that of the sample 64 per cent believed that access to buyers was an important location factor holding them in London (South East Joint Planning Study 1971).

required by small plants can be obtained at a central location but not elsewhere. Larger plants can very often internalize these external economies, and are therefore not tied to a core location. Vernon (1960) defined 'external economy industries' as those that needed to be close to other firms in order to make sales or to hold down costs, and showed that these industries were dominant in New York.[12] Moreover, even in these industries New York plants tended to be smaller than those outside. Location in the central core means that small manufacturing plants have easy access to the facilities offered there: skills, direct contact with suppliers, business and financial services, and external transport services. The only possibility under which small plants could obtain these external economies at a suburban location is if there is a highly developed, large, integrated industrial estate; very few of these, however, can offer specialist services comparable to those available in the city centre.

Shops. The overriding locational requirement for retail shops is a site that will attract custom. In general, the best sites will tend to be located near the point of greatest intracity accessibility.[13] However, there is obviously insufficient space available in the core to meet the needs of all retail establishments. Thus, competitive bidding for sites distributes shops among the sites available. Broadly speaking, shops with the highest turnover per square metre should outbid others and pre-empt the core sites. These will include department stores, the main branches of multiples specializing in general merchandise, consumer durables, clothes, jewellery, etc. and speciality shops. The latter need to serve a large population in order to thrive, and a central location enables them to draw custom from all over a metropolitan region. In most cases, they will be able to afford

12. In the City of London, the sole manufacturing industries are printing and publishing and specialized clothing production (Dunning, 1969).

13. Many of the models used to explain, and occasionally predict, retail location are of the accessibility type. See, for example Carroll (1955), Huff (1966), and Lakshmanan and Hansen (1965).

a central site. Firstly, their space requirements will be small. Secondly, site rentals and costs can vary widely within the centre between main shopping streets and sidestreets. The latter is frequently a satisfactory location for a speciality shop, for example coin and stamp shops, since these rarely need to rely on attracting the passing casual customer but have a regular clientele.

Shops selling more standardized products (food stores, newsagents, chemists, etc.) tend to adopt widely dispersed locations with a pattern approximating to the distribution of population. The spatial dispersion of shops reflects, among other things, frequency of custom. Shops selling goods bought daily will have to be near their customers, while the central shopping centres cater for weekly or more irregular shoppers. Some analysts have applied the 'high-order' and 'low-order' classifications derived from central place theory to retail shops (Berry, Barnum and Tennant, 1962; Berry, 1967). In these applications, the distribution of different types of shops in different parts of a city-region reflects the facts that consumers will travel further for 'high-order' goods and also that market area thresholds impose constraints on where shops may be located. *Ceteris paribus*, the larger the threshold market size for a particular group of commodities the more likely that the shop in question will adopt a central location. Central place models of retail location have two major drawbacks: they do not satisfactorily account for agglomeration and they have difficulty in predicting the location of new shops.

As with other economic activities, there are signs of decentralization in the retail trade. As the CBD expands with increasing city size, the floor area in retail use does not grow at a parallel rate. A marked feature of retail location trends in recent years has been the development of suburban shopping centres and also, especially in the United States, of out-of-town regional shopping centres. There has been a shift in favour of supermarkets and large-scale multiples, and establishments on this scale have usually needed to provide car parking facilities. This has made suburban locations more likely, partly on site cost grounds, partly because larger shops offering a greater variety are able to attract customers (especially by car) from greater distances. In most theories of retail location (and especially in gravity models), the *size* and variety of shopping facilities at a given location are an important attracting force. A large shopping complex can attract many more customers than two or three smaller centres having the same aggregate size. This explains why a peripherally located, regional shopping centre can attract enough viable custom if it offers sufficient variety in shopping opportunities, and if it provides the parking spaces required (Jones, 1969). Such a complex may consist, at one extreme, of a vast one-stop store under single ownership, or, at the other, of many shops of different types and sizes, some selling the same lines in competition. One reason why the large complex may be sited at a very peripheral location is to put distance between it and the city's main shopping centre and to reduce the overlap in their drawing power areas.

If size and variety attract custom, it is clear that shop location decisions are interdependent. Thus, a new shop that cannot afford a core site or an existing shop moving away from the centre will normally prefer to agglomerate near other shops in a suburban shopping centre, even if this means locating near competitors. Agglomeration is more efficient because it minimizes shoppers' travel costs and time. The minimization of travel costs is given a crucial role by Huff (1961) who argues that decentralization will tend to take place if it leads to a reduction in travel times. A related factor is increases in population density. This will encourage decentralization, firstly because traffic congestion as a function of density increases travel times and costs in the city centre, and secondly because the increases in residential density will tend to be concentrated in the suburbs thereby improving off-centre market potential.

Offices. Offices cling more closely to the central city than any other type of establishment, and they are also much more concentrated in large cities than in small urban centres. An increase in city size is associated with a proportionately larger increase in office space. This is partly because large cities perform a number of regional, national and international functions, partly because service sectors in general, and office employment in particular, are expanding. Within the large cities the preference of office establishments for a core location is very strong. Since the rentals for central office accommodation are much higher than in the suburbs (the latest LOB publicity suggests a differential between new rented Central London offices and comparable premises outside Greater London of £700 per employee per year[14]), the benefits of a core location must be regarded as substantial if firms continue to want offices there. One aspect of the situation is that the benefits of a central location, primarily external economies, are difficult to measure and are perhaps over-valued. These external economies include the ease of contact with other firms (especially the opportunity for face-to-face personal contacts), the possibility of better communication with other parts of the country (though in recent years suburban offices near the main routes to the airport have a higher degree of countrywide accessibility), the pool of clerical and secretarial labour available in the large city (though shortages may be acute for firms reluctant to 'poach') and the presence of commercial training facilities, spare capacity in the stock of office accommodation to meet the needs of expansion, access to business consultancy services,[15] and the prestige of a metropolitan address (Economist Intelligence Unit, 1964). These economies are important for many different kinds of office – banking and finance, insurance, the legal and accountancy professions, the sales organisations of manufacturing firms. The attractions of a core location are greater, *ceteris paribus*, for smaller firms and for specialists and central decision-making organizations. In Dunning's words:

What remains in the urban core is top of the hierarchy – an elite group of coordinators, decision-takers and policy-makers, with their

14. For details see Location of Offices Bureau (1970).

15. According to Dunning (1969), the sellers of information and ideas are the third largest employers in the City of London.

supporting staff; those who need to be in close proximity to others so as to negotiate, to converse, to gain or pass on information and ideas (1969).

Despite the attractions of the CBD for offices, this sector has not entirely escaped infection from the decentralization fever. In the seven years up to the end of March 1970, the Location of Offices Bureau with a vigorous advertising campaign had persuaded 906 office firms (involving more than 75,000 jobs) to decentralize from Central London, and there is world-wide evidence of a similar trend in other major metropolises. With modern means of communication and intercity transport by road or air, suburban locations can be as efficient as the core for many types of office. The larger firms normally find it easier to move. They figure disproportionately among the LOB's inquirers, and firms larger than 200 employees account for 62 per cent of the jobs decentralized. The smaller firms, generally speaking, remain tied to the CBD because of their need for linkages with other firms.[16] The importance of inter-dependence to many small offices means that they are most likely to move as part of a large scale office complex which aims to keep existing linkages uninterrupted; such a complex might internalize the external scale economies (Croft, 1969). In all cases, the preferred type of move is to a site within 60 minutes journey time from the city centre rather than to a smaller town or city further away (of the firms leaving Central London, 79 per cent moved less than 40 miles). Firms are also more likely to move from the core to the suburbs when external events force a response from them; for example, when a lease expires or the premises are due for demolition or an expansion programme cannot be achieved on the present site. Decentralization as a result of a rational reassessment of costs (rising accommodation rentals, higher wages or labour shortages, traffic congestion) is much less likely.

A recent development is the partial move in which routine office, records or service functions are decentralized while the

16. Wabe's research (1966) suggested that the expanding medium-sized firms were the best candidates for decentralization.

senior managers remain in the CBD. This usually involves some reorganization in office structure. Technical advances in communications systems help to maintain the necessary links between the routine and the decision-making branches. In a few cases, with modern intrafirm telecommunication links and improved air travel services, the routine office section may be moved hundreds of miles. In the majority of cases, however, the need for rapid personal contact remains, and partial moves are usually restricted to within a couple of hours travel time from the central city.

As in the case of other sectors, offices do not choose the location of their premises in a free market. The growth of office employment in a city may be dependent upon spare capacity in the stock of *existing* office accommodation, and this requires a prior release of land for commercial development by the planners. In Britain office developments in the South-East have been controlled since 1965. The 'office famine' in the suburbs around London has meant that there is often no suburban site to which the core office dependent on fairly easy access to Central London can move. At the same time, this general shortage of office space has pushed up rents in Central London itself. A firm willing to move may be trapped at a core location where it cannot escape from sharply rising costs. This is just another example of the general principle that non-market forces usually lead to locational inertia.

2 Urban Rent, Land Values and Spatial Structure

Urban rent and land values[1]
The nature of urban rent

The price of urban land, and the general level of urban rents, is determined like the price of any other commodity by demand and supply.

Since the supply of *central* urban land is essentially fixed, its value will be determined by the demand for central space. This makes it inevitable that core rents and land values rise over time unless sufficient urban establishments can find off-centre substitutes as productive as sites in the city centre to hold the demand for core land constant. Within an urban area as a whole, on the other hand, the supply of land can be increased, in the absence of green belt and planning controls, by annexation of more land on the city outskirts. Muth (1968a) has argued that the supply of urban land is moderately elastic, and is in fact equal to the negative of the agricultural demand elasticity for land.[2,3] Transport improvements can have a very

1. In the discussion of the nature of urban rent and the land values gradient that follows, no attention will be paid to the relationship between rent, site value and property value. Urban rent refers to the annual net return from a unit of land, though in practice the market rent level may be affected by other factors such as the term and conditions of the lease. The site value of a plot is the capitalized value of its expected future rental value. Thus, expectations and discount rates are relevant factors in the link between rent and land values. Since the demand for urban land is a derived demand related to the final demand for offices, shops, homes and other land uses, land values are in the long run related to the market prices of developed real properties.

2. Since the total amount of land in any area is fixed, the supply curve of urban land is this fixed amount less the agricultural demand curve for land.

3. The existence of a demand for agricultural land is important because it sets a floor below which the value of urban land will not fall.

important impact on urban land supply by extending the physical margin of urban development. Changes in the city's radius give rise to geometric increases in its area; an extension in the city boundary from 3 to 4 miles, for instance, will in a circular city increase the supply of urban land from 28·3 to 50·2 square miles. However, whether or not aggregate rents and land values move upwards or downwards depends upon the elasticity of demand for urban land. If this were very high, then any tendency for aggregate land values to fall after a transport improvement could be offset by increased consumption of space. However, it is probable that the price elasticity of demand for urban land is less than −1. In this case, urban land rents will tend to decline with transport improvements.[4]

The nature and source of urban rent is a subject that has given rise to confusion. This confusion probably stems from applying Ricardian-type agricultural rent theory to urban land. Apart from the minor qualification that geological considerations may affect the cost of building operations or the size of building which can be erected on a particular site, an urban site confers no advantages similar to superior fertility in agricultural rent. Agricultural rent at a particular location is, neglecting differences in fertility, equal to the difference between the transport costs to the market from that location and the costs from the marginal land. But it is misleading to explain urban rent in terms of transport cost savings, even though the complementarity of rent and transport costs figures prominently in theories of the household site selection process. Finally, the agricultural land market is purely competitive, whereas the market for urban land, as Chamberlin has shown (1956, Appendix D), contains monopolistic elements.

The nature of urban rent is perhaps clearer if we consider

4. Of course, other factors such as the growth of urban population and economic growth in general have led to rising land values in all the world's major cities in recent decades. Cities benefiting from marked transport improvements will therefore tend to exhibit below average increases in land values (see Goldberg, 1970b).

one type of urban land use – retail trade. In Chamberlin's words:

The rent of urban land is explained wholly, that of agricultural land partly, by the factor of location. . . . Urban rent arises because a piece of land can *sell* more – is better located within a certain trading area with reference to a *part* of the buyers. . . . The retail market . . . contains monopoly elements, for the factor of convenience differentiates the product spatially. . . . The rent on any urban site is an expression of the value of the monopoly privilege of providing retail services *at that particular place*. Competition among entrepreneurs to secure these monopoly gains is the force which puts them into the hands of the landlords.

In more generalized terms, urban rent is not a resource cost but a transfer payment. It is attributed to *urban productivity*, for being urban enables us 'to increase our productivity, and urban land values attempt to measure this increase. From this point of view, site rents are 'an index of urban progress' (Smith, 1969).

Why are urban sites more productive than others? The large size of the urban market offers greater revenue potential and the opportunity to gain economies of scale. In addition, agglomeration economies are often possible within a city. But if urban productivity is at the root of urban rent, what accounts for relative variations in urban rent levels between sites? In a formal sense, the explanation is the differences in productivity, and it is these differences which allow us to treat urban land, though of the same grade, as heterogeneous. In an urban context, variations in efficiency between sites can primarily be traced to differences in accessibility. In the words of the famous early land economist, Hurd (1903): 'Since value depends upon economic rent, and rent on location, and location on convenience, and convenience on nearness, we may eliminate the intermediate steps and say that value depends on nearness.'[5] However, accessibility divides into two quite distinct

5. Compare Brigham (1965, p. 326): 'Urban land has a value over and above its value in rural uses, because it affords relatively easy access to various necessary or desirable activities. If transportation were instantaneous and costless, then the urban population could spread over all

kinds: *general accessibility*, or nearness in travel costs to all other urban uses and facilities; and *special accessibility*, or nearness to particular types of complementary facilities. The latter, in contrast to the former, varies with the type of user. Special accessibility factors explain why certain types of use congregate together in different parts of the city.

It is interesting that central city land rents and values continue to soar despite the fact that the CBD's accessibility advantages are being increasingly whittled away – by rising traffic congestion costs and the development of other subcentres equally, or more, accessible. This suggests firstly that special accessibility, or complementarity of use and spatial proximity advantages for certain facilities, is more important than general accessibility, and secondly that there are other factors in urban productivity differentials besides accessibility. Some of these (for example agglomeration economies and external economies of scale) are subsumed under special accessibility; others, such as the prestige of a central city office or the amenity value attached to living in a certain area, are not. If we consider residential land values, for example, there are many influences additional to accessibility. Brigham's work (1964, 1965) is typical of research in this field. He adopted a multiple regression model in which he used measures of accessibility, amenity level and topography as independent variables, and also argued that historical factors (for example conditions prevailing at the point in time at which development takes place) and the value of the land in non-urban uses influences the demand for residential sites in an urban area, though these variables were not included in the tests. The instability of the regression coefficients from one set of data to another suggested that either these and/or other determinants needed to be included in the model. Another modification, particularly relevant to central land, is that the unit value of a

---

usable space and all land prices would be reduced to their approximate value in the best alternative use. But transportation is not instantaneous and costless, and since modern life requires the concentration of people in cities, urban land takes on a special accessibility value.'

site will depend on its size. There are large indivisibilities particularly in central city land uses (a department store, an office block, etc.), and consequently large sites tend to have considerably higher values per square metre than small ones do.

The land value gradient

If the major determinant of differences in urban rentals and land values within a city were accessibility, and if transportation were possible in all directions and transport cost–distance functions linear, then there should be a smooth land value gradient declining from the city centre towards the urban area boundary. Since these conditions do not hold in all respects, the shape of the gradient requires modification.

In the first place, the gradient does not fall towards zero even at distances that are virtually inaccessible to the city. At the edge of the urban area urban users have to compete for land with other uses, particularly agriculture. Thus, on city outskirts the rent level approximates that of the surrounding countryside. Moreover, unless there are vast differences between areas in the quality of agricultural land, it follows that the marginal land of each city (that is its floor level) will be priced about the same everywhere. The peak of land values will vary a lot between cities. As a generalization, the peak will be much higher in large cities. The demand for central land will be more intense there because of scale economies (both internal and external) in urban industries and because of higher incomes. It is important to note that intercity differentials in land value peaks cannot be explained by accessibility factors alone. The gap between land values at the central peak and at the urban-rural boundary can be very large indeed (Knos, 1962, Mills, 1967). If land values do vary so widely within a distance of 10–12 miles in a large metropolitan area (Mills suggests by a factor within the range ten to a hundred in the United States), this means large differentials in relative factor prices within cities. These lead to observed variations in capital–land ratios – tall office blocks and apartments in the CBD, and spread-out one floor production plants or low density single family dwellings in the suburbs (Mills, 1967).

It is most improbable therefore that the land value gradient has a constant slope or that land values can be expressed, even approximately, as a negative exponential function of radial distance. Instead, we find these very high peaks in the city centre with land values tending to decline rapidly towards the edge of the CBD. Further out, in the residential annulus land values will fall off much more slowly.[6] Near the outer boundary as the rural area is approached, the gradient may become even flatter, indeed almost horizontal.[7] These generalizations suggest that measurement of the slope of the land value gradient requires its division into at least three sections. In the residential annulus, the fall in land values will tend to be a slower than exponential decline. This is because households living at more central sites will tend to occupy smaller plots. This possibility of economizing on land for housing holds down demand, and hence increases in land values below what would otherwise be their levels as we move towards the city centre.

6. However, they will usually continue to decline. Indeed, if the observation that house prices decline with distance is valid, it can be shown theoretically that land values must also fall with distance. The absence of marked economies of scale in house-building means that cost differences between large and small builders cannot be very wide. Thus, the tendency for lower house prices on the outskirts of cities cannot be explained by the predominance of large building firms there. It follows that for locational equilibrium in the housing construction industry, land values must decline with distance.

7. A possible, and drastic, exception is in a city experiencing fast population growth. In this case, there may be a marked discontinuity in the land value gradient at the urban boundary. A wide gap between urban and rural land prices may emerge as a result of the activities of land speculators buying up land in anticipation of future urban development. The urban marginal land price may rise to an 'abnormal' level because the speculators are more interested in judging the future value of land than in maximizing its current income-earning capacity. Moreover, if they have large assets and/or a good credit rating they will tend to discount future returns at a low rate.

Apart from changes in slope, there are other distortions in the land value gradient. Diffusion of trip destinations, particularly decentralization of workplaces, tends to flatten it. But very often workplaces relocate, not to random points in the metropolitan area, but to secondary employment centres, and these will become high land value zones. Other local peaks will be found in the vicinity of suburban shopping centres and other sub-centres. Similarly, land values will be higher in different parts of the city according to whether areas have easier access to bus routes, suburban railway stations and main arteries in the urban road network than other areas equidistant from the city centre. Thus, if we plot the land value gradient along any ray from the city centre, the gradient will not decline continuously but will show small 'blips' where the ray cuts across a main road or passes through a sub-centre. These are not necessarily exceptions to the 'value reflects accessibility' hypothesis. The influence of the transport structure on the pattern of land values merely shows us that the transportation surface is not uniform and that isochrones are not circular; it does not require any departure from the view that general accessibility moulds land values. The minor peaks at sub-centres, on the other hand, can be explained in terms of special accessibility. As we have seen, special accessibility pulls certain types of activity together. When this is allowed for, it is quite possible to get a belt of low land values between two high values areas, or to find 'blips' distorting the gradient.

Legislation and planning controls may also influence the slope of the land gradient (Goodall, 1970). Density controls, for example, may restrict the type and intensity of development taking place on particular sites. They could raise or lower land values in a particular zone according to the elasticities of demand and supply of land for different uses and the impact of controls, if any, on neighbourhood effects and externalities. Another example is found in a metropolitan area comprising several rating authorities. Here, residential land values should tend to be higher, *ceteris paribus*, in areas with industry because of a lower rate poundage. Of course, this effect on residential land values could be offset by lower amenity value. A rather different point, implicit in the earlier discussion, is that the land value gradient will tend to be higher throughout its length in large and/or rich cities.

The land value gradient will change over time according to changes in accessibility between the city centre and different points within the city, shifts in location patterns of particular types of land, the rate of urban growth, the degree of intervention by planners, and many other factors. A study of Chicago (Yeates, 1965) compared 1960 with 1910. In 1910 land values within the CBD were very high but declined rapidly outside. By 1960, many of the older high-value areas had lost their value (though local variations were very wide), while new high-value zones had appeared in the outlying suburbs. Changes of this kind may well be explicable in accessibility terms. It is now generally accepted that in certain suburban locations accessibility indices are high compared with that in the central city, both for general accessibility (travel time to other parts of the city and proximity to *intercity* main roads) and for special accessibility (as a result of the development of sub-centres). Generalizations about the change in the land value gradient over time are difficult, particularly since CBD land values may continue to grow faster than elsewhere even in the face of relative deterioration in its accessibility. It is clear, however, that the spatial structure of land values becomes much more complex so that the gradient itself becomes more irregular with signs of more ridges and valleys. Also, with the possible exception of near the middle of the CBD, the slope of the gradient will tend to become less steep.

Finally, it may be of some relevance to refer to the pattern of land values in and around the London metropolitan area.[8] Land values in the central city are, of course, very high. Between a 5 and 10 miles radius, however, there is a very rapid fall. Beyond this, land values decline much more

8. The following observations are mainly drawn from the National Building Agency (1968). For more information of land values in London and the south-east in the early 1960s, see McAuslan (1966).

slowly. At a radius of 20–25 miles, land values actually begin to rise again. Although this is inconsistent with the above analysis, the paradox is easily explained. The rise in land rents and values reflects pressure on the amount of land available for development. At this distance from Central London, the Green Belt absorbs a great deal of land, and the designation of land as areas of interest and scenic beauty has put building sites at a premium. At the same time, the movement in land values reflects the willingness of commuters to tolerate longer journeys to work in return for a more pleasant living environment (that is amenity outweighs accessibility). In the south-east region as a whole, this qualification scarcely disturbs the generalization that land values are higher the greater the proximity and the better the commuting access to Central London. The main exception, in addition to that already noted, is found in desirable coastal resorts within reasonable travelling distance from London. Empirical evidence for the south-east also supports the tendency for land values to affect intensity of land use, for there is a clear positive relationship between the price of land and residential density.

Density gradients

In a city with a single centre, space will be used most intensively at the core and the density of use will tend to fall off in all directions with increasing distance from it. In such cities radial gradients can be estimated for several phenomena: population density, urban land values (as discussed above), employment per acre of land occupied, etc. Analysis of urban population densities has received the most attention since Clark (1951) rediscovered a relationship propounded sixty years earlier by Bleicher (1892). The basic hypothesis is that population density is a negative exponential function of radial distance:

$$P_d = P_o \, e^{-bd}$$

where P_d equals the gross residential population density in persons/acre, and P_o is the residential population density at the city centre, or rather, in view of the fact that commercial and public buildings will occupy much of the CBD, the hypothetical density obtained from extrapolating observed densities inwards. In this equation, e is the Napierian logarithmic base (2·718), b is the slope of the density gradient and d is the radial distance from the city-centre. P_d and d are variables, e is a constant and P_o and b are parameters fixed for each city at any given time.[9]

Although the density gradient is a purely descriptive measure, it reflects the influence of behavioural characteristics and economic forces. This is most clearly seen in considering the determinants of the b coefficient. First, however, a comment on the coefficient itself. A constant value for b is usually assumed; allowing it to vary from zone to zone would make the formula cumbersome, giving rise to a curvilinear set of density gradients instead of a single smooth curve for each city. For instance, Hoover (1968) has reported work by B. Newling which expresses the logarithm of density as a *quadratic* rather than a linear function of radial distance. The advantage of this modification is that it allows for the 'caving in' of the density gradient in the CBD and for off-centre peaks.

The slope of the density gradient (b) is of course a measure of the spread of the city. High transport costs, for example, will mean a high value for b. An old-established city (with a large centrally situated housing stock) or one with a centralized employment distribution will also tend to have a steep gradient. Size, fast growth and high incomes, on the other hand, should result in relatively flat slopes. Moreover, efficient transport such as relatively cheap electric rail systems (Sydney, Chicago, London, Osaka, etc.) or car-dominated cities (for example Los Angeles) will also lead to low bs. The slope of the gradient has declined over time and this has been accompanied by a decline in central densities. This is possible despite ex-

9. If we ignore the fact that central sites will be pre-empted by non-residential uses, integration yields a total urban population of $2\pi P_o b^{-2}$.

panding city populations because a slow decline in density in the central and inner zones has gone along with rapid increases in the outer zones, with each zone stabilizing at a lower density than the adjacent inner one. A number of years ago, a study of Philadelphia by Blumenfeld (1954) indicated that the zone of fastest growth, or in his terminology the 'crest of the wave of metropolitan expansion', moves outward in a regular fashion. It is clear that b may vary considerably from city to city.[10] The value for the other parameter, P_o or central density, is largely determined by the economic conditions prevailing at the time the city was established, and is then subject to inertia. Among the relevant economic conditions are the transport network, the level of income and the production technology. Berry (Berry, Simmons and Tennant, 1963) has even argued that a city's population and age are sufficient to predict its density distribution.

Patterns of household behaviour underlie these parameters. In some Continental cities for instance, where workers prefer to return home for their midday meal, central densities will be high and the gradient will be steep. The slope of the gradient will depend in fact on how households trade off accessibility for more space, which in turn will be influenced by income levels, family composition and the stage of the family cycle, environmental preferences and the relative pull of city amenities compared with easy access to open country. The determinants of residential location decisions are still unclear, and the value of b merely generalizes the consequences of thousands of micro-decisions.[11]

The density gradient concept is not confined to analysis of gross urban population densities. A better fit can be obtained for *net* residential densities (that is population per acre of land *in residential use* excluding streets, non-residential sites

10. See Clark (1967, pp. 349–50), for empirical estimates of b for a large number of world cities, and Muth (1961, p. 211), for estimates of many cities in the United States.

11. See ch. 1, pp. 18–28. One of the implications of the household location models suggested in that chapter is that the density gradient will not be smooth in all directions.

and open spaces[12]). It is also possible to derive a gradient for the spatial distribution of the daytime population as opposed to residential population; the centralization of employment opportunities means a higher peak and a steeper slope. An early study by Duncan (1957), using data on Chicago in 1951, found a gradient for manufacturing employees per unit area of land occupied, though with a much flatter slope than for residential densities. Decentralization of manufacturing over the past twenty years, however, may have obliterated this particular gradient. Echenique (1968) found similar evidence of a negative exponential distance function for his floor-space ratio (that is the amount of floor area divided by the land area). Land values may reveal the same kind of exponential gradient,[13] as may house prices if we standardize for quality and size of house and amenity value of location.

We must be careful not to put too much strain on the density gradient as a measure of urban structure. For one thing, it implies radial symmetry. It is apparent that many cities cannot spread uniformly in all directions, for reasons such as topographical constraints or the existence of a cheap but skeletal public transport system. Secondly, in modern cities it is becoming increasingly apparent that economic and social activities do not focus only on a single centre but on several sub-centres scattered over the urban region. These qualifications are not necessarily critical. It has already been suggested how the formula might be adjusted to take them into account, while the leading analyst of urban residential patterns (Muth, 1968a, p. 300) has concluded that 'a negative exponential pattern of gross population densities in relation to distance is as good an approximation to actual patterns as any other'.

The simplest model of spatial structure: concentric zones
Changes in the structure of cities over the past few decades make schematic models of spatial structure most unsatisfac-

12. It is worth pointing out that if hotels are counted as a residential use, we even get a true net density peak in the CBD.

13. Mills (1969) suggested a double-log rather than an exponential relationship.

tory when subject to close scrutiny. These changes include technological advances in industry and services, transport improvements, suburbanization, the development of sub-centres competing in some respects with the CBD, greater flexibility in choice of location for most activities, a more active pursuit of urban planning goals, and many others. It would be reasonable to expect the simplest models of spatial structure to suffer most. Paradoxically, however, it is the refinements and the alternatives that now seem of little value. The faults of the original simplistic models still remain; indeed, if anything, they are a little more serious. But behind the simplicity there lies a core of truth sufficient to enable these models to enhance our understanding of even the most modern cities. The gap between the model and the reality may be a very wide one, but it can be bridged by relaxing some of the assumptions and taking account of new variables.

In making these comments, I have one long-established and widely discussed model in mind. This is the concentric zone model. This derives from ideas on the theory of urban land use and urban rent associated with von Thünen, Haig, Burgess and Ratcliff, while the discussion of urban rent and land use by more recent analysts such as Alonso and Wingo can also be used to buttress some of the key points even though they would undoubtedly repudiate the model itself. The relationship between the operation of a competitive urban land market, rent gradients and the derivation of a concentric zonal structure can be shown by starting from two assumptions: a hypothetical city in which the central point offers maximum accessibility, and accessibility declines with distance and the utility of firms and households depends upon accessibility.[14] Thus, for firms, revenue is assumed to be maximized at the city centre, while accessibility is important for households because it minimizes the costs and time involved in travel to work, to the shops and to other establishments with which households

14. This is an assumption of the model rather than a statement of fact. My strong reservations on travel minimization, as a determinant of the household location decision, were discussed in ch. 1, pp. 19–24.

make contact. Competition for sites offering accessibility bids up urban rent levels, and urban establishments are content to pay more for central sites because they save transport costs by locating there. It follows that rents will fall with distance from the city centre, thereby yielding a rent gradient.

How this gives rise to a concentric zone structure of land use can be shown as follows. The utility an economic activity

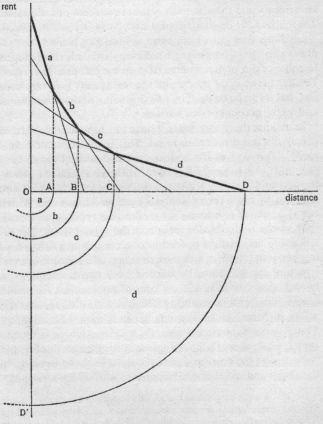

Figure 1

receives from occupying a site can be measured by the rent that the activity is willing to pay for the land. The greater the utility obtained, the more rent an activity will be prepared to pay. Assuming a competitive urban land market, bidding for land ensures that each site is occupied by its highest and best use. If utility is measured by rent (under competition any surplus in excess of costs will accrue to the landlord) and given our assumption that utility (accessibility) falls with distance from the city centre, we obtain a concentric circular pattern of land use. This is seen in Fig. 1. We can draw up for any set of activities, a set of rent functions showing how the rent which each is willing to pay falls with distance. For pedagogic purposes, let us assume only four competing uses (*a*, *b*, *c*, *d*) and that rent-distance functions are linear. The four rent functions are superimposed on each other in the diagram. This results in a spatial pattern with the functions arranged in descending order of steepness. Since competition ensures that the 'highest and best' use occupies any particular site, it is clear that activity *a* outcompetes all other activities between O and A, *b* dominates between A and B, *c* between B and C, while *d* occupies the peripheral sites between C and D. The overall rent gradient of the city is shown by the bold line. If the model is translated from linear to areal terms by rotating OD about O, as in the lower part of Fig. 1, we obtain a concentric zonal pattern of land use with activity *a* located in the central zone, *b* in the inner ring, *c* in the outer ring, BC, and *d* in the peripheral zone CD.

Furthermore, if firms (or households) in each sector are homogeneous, the concentric zones will spatially segregate different types of activity. Thus, for example, we might find CBD activities (department stores, offices, hotels, theatres, etc.) in the central core, wholesaling and light manufacturing in the innermost ring, slum dwellings in the next ring[15], and

15. The latter two zones are sometimes grouped together as the 'zone of transition', with other supplementary activities intermingled. Preston (1966, p. 236) has described this zone as follows: 'Peripheral to the CBD of the city there exists a transition zone. This zone embraces a large portion of the so-called "grey area" and usually presents serious problems.

middle-income and then upper-income dwellings further out. The affinity between this view of urban spatial structure and the rural land use zonal model of von Thünen has often been noted. The activities quoted are treated as key locational types. The main omission is heavy industry which (because of substantial space demands, transport access to main trunk roads, and input–output relations oriented to the rest of the world rather than to the city) is unlikely to choose a location within the city.

In no real-world city can we find a pattern of land use and spatial structure that closely corresponds with the concentric zone schema. The modifications needed to the model are almost numberless. Here, we shall refer only to the most widespread and most important.

For instance, the assumptions of the model about locational behaviour may conflict drastically with reality. We have seen that the location decisions of households may have little to do with a desire for accessibility, and this holds for certain kinds of non-residential establishments too. Moreover, units within a sector may be heterogeneous (production functions differ among shops, and among city factories even in the same industry; households differ according to income, class, size, car

---

It is typified by mixed land use, ageing structures, general instability and change, and by a wide range in type and quality of functions. The zone's housing exhibits all degrees of obsolescence; many of its public facilities, ribbon-shopping concentrations, and industrial-wholesale-storage districts are outmoded and suffer from high vacancy rates and the presence of numerous marginal operations. Population, while normally either holding its own or increasing numerically, is trending toward ethnic or racial aggregation and at the same time toward lower education and income levels. Such conditions appear to exist because the zone, in addition to the burden of obsolescence and civic scorn, possesses neither the locational advantages of a CBD nor conditions which are readily adaptable to a widely desirable pattern of residential living. Consequently, the transition zone lies neglected by both public and private enterprise.' The zone separates the retail and business heart of the city from surrounding tracts of homogeneous land use, usually residential, and it is typically three times as large as the CBD.

ownership, etc.), and this heterogeneity may be important in determining location. There may be several equally good locations for a household or firm, and the end result may vary widely from the spatial segregation implied in the model just outlined. Similarly, interdependence among locations has to be taken into account. Whereas some activities find it beneficial to agglomerate, others prefer to locate so as to corner a sheltered market area. Thus, the rent function of a firm may not be independent of the spatial pattern of firms already in the industry. As far as retail trade is concerned, application of an intraurban central place model can explain why some shops may seek a core location while others are content with a suburban site. It is true that recognition of heterogeneity of establishments as a fact of importance for urban location patterns does not necessarily completely destroy a concentric zone model *per se*, provided we treat each firm as a separate activity. But since many activities prefer to agglomerate together rather than spread themselves around the city within a very narrow ring, we are then likely to find each ring containing a mixed group of activities and very marked distortions of the neat, separated patterns of homogeneous land use implied in the concentric zone model.

Most cities are not circular, even as an approximation. The main reason for this is topographical barriers, such as seas, rivers or hills. Thus, many coastal cities are semicircular in shape. Provided the non-urbanized sections are fairly regular in shape (for example a semicircle, or a pie-shaped wedge), the model can take them into account by reducing the area of urban space by an appropriate amount.

Even in a circular city in which all units locate to maximize accessibility, the concentric theory may not hold. This is because in a modern city in which motor vehicles are an important transport mode, it is no longer clear that the city centre is the point of maximum accessibility. Travelling time and transport costs on the roads are a function of traffic volume, and congestion in the city centre can mean a lower degree of accessibility. The fact that urban rents continue to be at their highest level in the core suggests that rents are in fact not determined by accessibility alone. Moreover, regardless of whether public or private transport predominates, the existence of radial transport routes means that accessibility at any given radius from the CBD will be greater near to the main arteries than at a distance from them. The concentric zone model assumes an ubiquitous transportation surface, and radial transport routes pull the circle into something similar to a star shape. On the question of accessibility generally, the model implicitly assumes that no substitution is possible between transportation and other inputs. In effect, it assumes that each establishment makes a fixed number of trips at a given unit journey cost between its site and the city centre. In reality, if the city centre is inaccessible, a firm will try to find ways of reducing the number of journeys and contacts and/or to substitute a more convenient alternative destination. The first may be achieved by altering its input and output structure, the possibility of the second arises because in a large modern metropolis the monopoly power of the core is not unlimited.

This raises an important characteristic of modern cities, the presence of important sub-centres subsidiary to and competing with the CBD.[16] These sub-centres can arise for several reasons. They may be explicable in terms of intrametropolitan central place analysis, especially when the growth of the city has absorbed old-established small urban centres. They may reflect the heavy space requirements of certain strategic activities

16. The description of the spatial structure of a modern city in terms of 'multiple nuclei' was first suggested by Harris and Ullman (1945). I would argue that this represents an important modification of the concentric zone theory rather than an alternative or a refutation, since the rent gradients and the concentric rings will tend to form around each nucleus. Similarly, Hoyt's radial sector hypothesis (1939) in which he argued growth will take place in certain sectors of, rather than throughout, a concentric ring can be explained by factors already mentioned, such as the tendency for some activities to cluster within a small space rather than to disperse all over the city, attraction and repulsion between certain kinds of activity, topographical constraints and the sequential development of transport facilities. Once again, it can be regarded as a qualification to rather than a refutation of a concentric zone structure.

- Simplions Models - but simplify don't explain
- nor the feel of the city
- Accessability not major - needs peoples
whims likely
Urban Rent, Land Values and Spatial Structure 63

(airports, universities, etc.) which need large but compact sites that are too expensive or are impossible to obtain near the central core; these activities also act as an attracting force for others. Service establishments catering for a market which is itself found only in certain parts of the city (for instance, high-income households) will also tend to locate at off-centre sites. The scarcity of core sites, and the possibility of reduced accessibility there, may lead in very large cities to the development of secondary office zones and suburban shopping centres which will form new nuclei. A major city nowadays is bound to contain several sub-centres each of which will be characterized by rents higher than in their surrounding area. While these localized rent peaks remain lower than that found in the central core, they mean a serious distortion to the concentric zone schema. The rent gradient from the city centre will be irregular with hillocks and craters rather than smooth, while the areal pattern will look rather like the ripples on a lake after a shower of pebbles of different size.

Finally, the concentric zone model as initially described relies rather heavily on the notion of competitive bidding for sites in market conditions. But the urban land market does not operate freely. Rigidities include locational inertia, long leases and pre-emption of sites by suboptimal uses. Zoning regulations, restrictions on planning permission, density controls, rent restrictions and other forms of intervention in the working of the market have quite an important influence. We have also to consider the activities of speculators for urban land who may buy up sites for future development but lease them to inferior uses on a temporary basis at rents below the long-run market level.

All these qualifications make it abundantly clear that the concentric zone model is, in its original form, a very poor representation of the spatial structure of a modern city. But a major aim of a theory should not be the slavish representation of reality which is a chimera; it should be to increase our understanding of a complicated phenomenon by means of simplification and generalization. The central concepts of the

but oversimplification

concentric zone analysis – the importance of accessibility, competitive bidding for central sites, the rent gradient, the emergence of a spatial pattern of land use – are necessary to comprehend the spatial structure of land values, rents and land use in any modern city. Without the aid of these or similar concepts, the city may, in Haig's words, appear to be 'without rhyme or reason, a confused and baffling welter of anomalies and paradoxes' while the assignment of land to different uses may seem 'to the superficial observer to have been made by the Mad Hatter at Alice's tea party' (1926).

Dynamics of urban spatial structure

There is not much point in giving a great deal of attention to static models of spatial equilibrium in the city, since the urban economy is characterized by dynamism and chance. As many observers have pointed out, for example Dyckman (1964), to treat the city as a closed system in equilibrium, immune from outside shocks, will make for bad planning and lead to a failure to understand what makes the city tick. Of course, static equilibrium analysis is easier and there are serious obstacles in the way of dynamic analysis of the city. Harris (1965) has explained how these obstacles have been obviated. First, recursive models involving step-wise projections are widely used in which the changes taking place in a given period depend on the state of the system at the beginning of the period. Secondly, to make up for the scarcity of time-series data, time is injected into these models by introducing specified amounts of exogenous variables such as population change, in-migration, economic growth and income expansion. Urban simulation models are usually moulded on these lines.

Most spatial structure models can be dynamized to a greater or lesser degree. The concentric zone theory discussed above, for instance, can be expanded to take account of urban growth. Growth will lead to a pushing out and widening of concentric zones of activity, and land uses dominant in one ring will tend to spread into the next outer ring by a process which the urban ecologists have called 'invasion-succession'.

But the reservations to the concentric zone models already noted are strongly reinforced in a dynamic context. A growth in office and service employment, for example, is as likely to manifest itself in the development of a secondary office/ shopping centre as in an outward spread of the CBD.

We are still a long way off from complete understanding of the spatial consequences of urban change.[17] Some insight can be gained from empirical observations of what happens as growth occurs in individual cities, but patterns can vary between cities and generalization is difficult. The alternative – the urban modelling approach – is also very useful, but the results are often disappointing. These models frequently over-emphasize land use conversion. In a brave attempt to get away from mechanistic and deterministic change and to get closer to a behavioural system, and hence to focus on the individual decision-makers on the urban scene, they often use allocation criteria based on probability theory, but the gains tend to be outweighed by lack of specificity and vagueness in their predictions. Above all, the compromise between model sophistication and ease of testing is invariably an uneasy one. The testable models are too crude, while the models approaching reality are too cumbersome in their data requirements to test.

Some spatial characteristics of urban expansion are obvious and fairly universal. Urban growth will normally be associated with both upward and outward expansion. Near the city centre, low structures will tend to be replaced by higher ones and there will be attempts to encroach on open spaces and build on any spare plots. Central densities (with the probable exception of residential density) will rise, and central land will be used more intensively. At the same time, however, the settled urban area will expand outwards. One of the main reasons for this is that efficient production of goods requires new land as an input. Another is that the provision of new housing for an expanding city population will require (and be cheaper on)

17. This section is concerned with the spatial implications of urban growth and change and not with the broader non-spatial aspects of economic growth and the city which are analysed in ch. 3.

new land, especially if, as is often the case, rising income levels are associated with a demand for more living space. Thus, although density gradients tend to become higher near the city centre, they also become flatter. In fact, the rate of increase in densities is usually highest near the boundary of the urban area. This is especially marked in the case of population densities, and it has been shown that the zone of fastest population growth, or the 'crest of the wave of metropolitan expansion', moves outward over time (Blumenfeld, 1954, 1964). This observation implies and gives undue emphasis to a concentric or ring pattern of growth. In some instances, expansion of a settled area may take quite different forms – for instance, sector or pie-slice growth, axial or finger growth extending settlement along radial transport routes, or suburban or satellite growth in which islands of settlement are created in advance of the outward spread of the main urbanized area.

Urban growth on a substantial scale invariably creates problems for the CBD, and may require some modification in its role and functions. Firstly, the CBD may change in shape. A typical example is where the main shopping centre bulges out towards the better residential districts. Secondly, the direction of expansion in the urban area may reduce the locational advantages of the CBD. Since most cities are not circular and some are faced with topographical barriers on one side (for example the sea), growth tends to occur in one direction only and the CBD ceases to be as centrally situated as when the city was smaller in size. Combined with other tendencies associated with rising central densities (congestion, environmental nuisances, soaring central land prices, the scarcity of large sites), this fact tends to weaken the competitive power of the CBD. Sometimes, this debilitation is accentuated by an extensive grey area or 'zone of transition' which cuts off the CBD from the rest of the urban region.[18] The decline in central city dominance may coincide with and be aggravated by increased transport efficiency which enables peripheral locations

18. Hence, redevelopment of this zone is often vital to a resurgence of the strength of the CBD.

to be more easily substituted for central locations (Guttenberg, 1960), though such improvements are unlikely to eliminate the economic significance of distance in urban structure altogether.

Two other general aspects of change in the spatial structure of contemporary cities, the development of sub-centres and the growth of suburbanization, are of course the obverse of this modified role of the CBD.[19] Sub-centres develop because with extensive urbanization and increases in scale it is no longer efficient to service a large city from one core. Voorhees (1968) has argued that a population increment of 100,000 can justify an additional centre to serve it, while Netzer (1970) has even suggested that an active planning policy to develop subcentres, preferably located at radial and crosstown transport intersections, is desirable to prevent some of the dangers of central congestion and the higgledy-piggledy sprawl of 'spread city'.[20] Candidates for the title of sub-centre include intraurban transport junctions, secondary business zones, large establishments such as hospitals or universities, and suburban shopping centres. The development of the latter, as predicted by application of the hierarchical principles of a central place model, is inevitable in a large city since it becomes difficult to reach the main shopping centre from a distance of, say, more than six miles away. At such distances, centres are likely to find sufficient population and purchasing power within their potential sphere of influence to create a threshold market size. Ullman (1962, p. 22) summed up the subcentring phenomenon as follows:

The metropolis of today and increasingly in the future is not only one city, but a federation of general and special centres. As such it is likely to have several hearts better located than one, and basically

19. Vance (1964) has even argued that the modern city is non-centric and that the CBD, rather than being an attracting force, is ignored. Most observers regard this as an extreme view.

20. Such a policy could involve firstly, coordination of public investment decisions, secondly modification of transportation plans and networks, and thirdly revision of land use controls so as to allow development of the kind required to take place.

will be better off because of reduction in travel time, congestion, and utilization of better sites.

The growth of sub-centres has important consequences for the structure of urban land use leading to a much more elaborated differentiated pattern and to a more spatial division of labour and specialization of functions.

Suburbanization tendencies affect not only people and manufacturing industry but service industries and other activities too. There has been a measure of disagreement about whether jobs started to decentralize before people or vice versa. There is probably no unique sequence but variations in experience from city to city and over time. In any event, speculation is idle. There are many separate reasons why both people and industries might wish to relocate from the central city (though not all of these are a consequence of urban growth), and once one moves out it tends to attract the other. This interdependence reinforces decentralization trends.

Strictly speaking, a distinction needs to be made between decentralization and suburbanization. Decentralization is a more general term that refers to relocation from the CBD and can cover, among other things, movement to one of the sub-centres discussed above. Decentralization is probably most easily measured by changes in the shape and slope of density gradients (residential population and employment of different types) over time. Suburbanization, on the other hand, usually means movement to a satellite or suburb *outside* the central city, whereas sub-centres can and do develop within it. A suburb has been defined as an urbanized nucleus (meaning an area of substantial population density, a preponderance of non-rural occupations and urban life styles) located outside but accessible to a central city. Although often politically independent, it is economically and psychologically linked with services and facilities provided by the metropolis. While there is a danger in overemphasizing the polarity between the two, residential suburbs can be distinguished from industrial satellites. The former tend to grow faster. The latter develop because certain, typically manufacturing, functions can be carried out more efficiently away from the central city. They enjoy space advantages, often the journey to work is shorter, yet they remain accessible to urban services. Finally, urban sprawl is a more formless type of decentralization, affecting population more than industries. Although sprawl is not necessarily an evil in itself, it frequently shows undesirable characteristics: ribbon development with a boring and unattractive physical appearance; no central place with which people can identify themselves and a consequent lack of community feeling; high public service and transport costs, and poor access to many urban facilities; and in some countries, such as the United States but not in the United Kingdom, extravagant consumption of land and a preponderance of detached low-density dwellings.

There have been many suggested causes of suburbanization and decentralization. The evidence to assess the most important of these influences is often conflicting. Here we do no more than list some of the widely quoted explanations. In this context, the important point is that the factors behind suburbanization are not necessarily traceable to the consequences of the *urban* growth process itself. Some are due to technological change, particularly the role of transport improvements which have reduced the need for agglomeration, narrowed intraurban land value differentials and probably resulted in amenity being more important than access as a location determinant. Others are partly explained by urban growth, partly by other influences the separate effects of which are virtually impossible to unravel. For example, consider the movement of higher income families from the central city to the suburbs. It is clear that one element in the situation has been the effects of urban growth on the characteristics of the central city leading to overcrowding in poor quality old housing structures; the natural tendency for residential segregation has seen to the rest (though often reinforced by higher property tax rates). On the other hand, expanding incomes, more leisure and increased car ownership have been associated with greater space demands and preferences for new houses primarily found at the city outskirts. In regard to industry, while high central congestion costs and shortages of core sites have been significant decentralizing forces linked with urban growth, technological changes in this century (cheap electric power, development of the telephone network permitting peripheral location of production plants, and continued central location of managerial functions) have been more or less independent of urban growth.

Two final comments. Decentralization is no recent phenomenon. In New York, for example, the process can be traced back as far as the 1850s. Indeed, Schnore (1957) suggested that decentralization trends could be treated as an index of a city's maturity. Secondly, it has repercussions on urban transport flows. As decentralization occurs, the intraurban flow of traffic becomes much more complex with more radial traffic and cross-commuting. Thus, changes in location and in transport are interdependent, and have strong implications for urban spatial structure.

Spatial allocation models

Urban land use, transportation and planning models have been a major growth industry in the past decade, particularly in the United States and more recently, and to a lesser extent, in the United Kingdom and elsewhere. Here we are concerned with one branch of these models, spatial allocation models. These attempt to distribute units of growth (people, firms, activities) among different parts of a metropolitan area with the aid of allocation criteria, behavioural assumptions or optimal decision rules or in line with the previous pattern of development.[21] Sometimes they deal with the full range of urban activities, but frequently they analyse only one sector, for instance, the Penn–Jersey (Herbert and Stevens, 1960), the North Carolina, (Donnelly, Chapin and Weiss, 1964) and San Francisco (Arthur D. Little, Inc., 1966) models of the residential sector or the Baltimore (Lakshmanan and Hansen, 1965)

21. There is no space to present a detailed survey of these models here. Several of them are analysed in Harris (1965), or summarized in Lowry (1967). Further references are given in Bourne (1969).

and Chicago (Berry, 1965) models of retail structure. In the latter case, these are in effect sub-models which need to be incorporated in a more comprehensive framework if city spatial structure is to be examined. In addition, many of the more general models include a component, or submodel, to represent the transport system. This inclusion reflects the importance of accessibility and transport costs on urban location.

The models draw upon a variety of contrasting approaches. Some simulate the activities of individual decision-makers in the urban land market (again the North Carolina model is a good example), some draw upon accessibility notions, gravity models and intervening opportunity models (Row and Jurkat, 1959; Lakshmanan and Hansen, 1965; Lathrop and Hamburg, 1965; Hansen, 1959), others use a recursive approach in which development in one period is influenced by the path of previous development (Hill, 1965, Steger, 1965), and yet others adopt linear programming formulations (Herbert and Stevens, 1960, Schlager, 1965). Although a comprehensive model should integrate land use and location, many of the models have a bias one way or the other. Thus, while those developed by Hamburg, Donnelly, Chapin and Weiss, Schlager and Bourne (1969), for example, emphasize land use succession and conversion, others (Hill, 1965; Lowry, 1964) are primarily location oriented. Although most of the models were constructed by planners (and one or two by geographers), their content and mechanisms do not appear strange to the economist. Even so, discussion of these simulations will not detain us for long.

The hasty dismissal of urban models is not intended to imply that they are useless. On the contrary, they can be very useful indeed particularly to the urban planner. What they do not do, however, is describe, predict and satisfactorily explain how the spatial structure of the city changes during the process of urban growth. Although several of them present a passable simulation of the absorption of peripheral land into urban land use, most ignore the crucial changes that take place in the central core.[22] Despite the fact that the models have proved very

22. Bourne's model is a rare exception.

difficult to test[23] because of the number of variables and heavy data requirements, their spatial allocation criteria tend to be either crudely mechanistic or random and pay little attention to the complexities of urban location decisions. No urban model to my knowledge explains the sub-centring phenomenon which is so important in urban spatial growth; none gives due attention to forces of agglomeration and deglomeration. Interdependence and feedback are similarly neglected. Most serious of all, none of the urban models are really dynamic. For the time variable there is substituted physical increments in exogenous variables such as population and the stock of buildings. These are handled either by one-shot projections (an 'instant metropolis') or by step-wise projections (recursive models). In neither case is there any serious possibility of accommodating the varied responses of individual decision-makers to urban change.

Economics of racial housing segregation

It would be a glaring omission in any book on urban economics not to mention racial segregation in housing. In the United States, where the problem is most acute, many of the social and economic problems created by city life derive from the presence of black ghettos. Residential segregation is an important aspect of the spatial structure of the city. The spatial separation and mutual repulsion of high income residences, typically located in the suburbs, and low income slums, typically located in or near the central city, have already been noted. Under a market system of allocating houses, residential segregation is probably inevitable since where people live depends very much on the rent or house price they pay. Also, it is socially based since people choose their neighbours according to desirable personal and social attributes, use income as an

23. Consider Lowry's remark on the Arthur D. Little San Francisco model: 'In idle moments I have tried to imagine the expression on the face of the staff demographer when he was asked to contribute, for each biennium of an 18-year forecasting interval, a prediction of the numbers of households in each of 114 socio-economic categories' (1967, p. 46).

index of these attributes and treat housing value as a proxy for neighbours' unknown income. Residential segregation is an important contributor to many urban problems – imbalance in urban fiscal systems, excessive commuting, persistence of unemployment and poverty. In American cities, for instance, residential segregation and unemployment are mutually reinforcing. Unemployment means that many central ghetto residents could not afford to gain access to housing outside the ghetto. On the other hand, living in the central ghetto makes it difficult for them to share in the growth of employment opportunities in the suburbs, partly because of the costliness and/or inadequacy of transport, partly because of ignorance of job vacancies available in the distant suburbs.

Residential segregation will emerge, in the absence of chequer-board residential land use zoning or other planning controls, as a result of income and occupational differences alone. When the racial ingredient is added, the situation is aggravated. Racial housing segregation cannot be explained, except to a slight degree, by lower economic status (that is income and occupational differentials). Evidence in both the United States and Britain (Lieberson, 1963; Doherty, 1969) makes it clear that black populations are more segregated than other non-indigenous nationalities and ethnic groups. Taeuber and Taeuber (1965) have shown that in over one half of American cities about 90 per cent of the Negro population would have to move to new homes in order to be spatially distributed in the same way as whites.

The arguments used against attempts to reduce this high degree of housing segregation are often emotive rather than soundly based. For instance, consider the proposition that once Negroes gain access to a 'white' neighbourhood it rapidly becomes Negro. This needs qualification, since the transition of an area does not happen automatically but is dependent upon certain conditions. Thompson (1965) for example, outlined a 'segregation model' in which the rate at which the Negro-white residential boundary moves outwards is a function of the rate of Negro in-migration. This, in turn, is a function of job opportunities and housing conditions (as measured by room occupancy rates and relative rents for housing of a given quality). Furthermore, white resistance at the border will accentuate overcrowding in the Negro areas while expectations of eventual defeat may induce white residents to cut back their maintenance expenditures. As a result, urban blight will be aggravated and urban renewal made more difficult. Thus, whether an invaded area is transformed into an all-black area or not depends on many complex factors, some economic (in-migration rates, the rate of job expansion) but others are social and psychological (for example white resident attitudes and expectations).

Another argument, in many circumstances mythical, is that Negro occupancy harms property values. Laurenti (1960), however, showed that price changes could be in either direction in an invaded area, and calculated that the odds were four to one that house prices would keep up with or be greater than prices in a comparable all-white area. Of course, this could well reflect the pressures of Negro demand for housing once a hitherto excluded housing area became available to them. If forces making for housing segregation are strong, the white and the non-white housing markets may be treated almost as independent, where the price level in the non-white housing market is determined by the limited supply of the housing stock open to non-whites and the level of non-white demand. This could explain why Negroes might have to pay high rents for poor housing. If as a result of discrimination Negroes are confined to only limited segments of the housing market, competition for this limited supply will bid up its price, regardless of its quality.

If Negro segregation cannot be explained in terms of their lower economic status, what causes it? How far is it due to overt discrimination, or can it be explained by other factors? Muth (1969) gives an interesting discussion of this question. He rejects both the 'unique aversion' theory, that is that landlords and estate agents have a special aversion to dealing with non-whites, and the 'collusion hypothesis', that is that estate agents limit the range of properties open to Negroes in order to profit from higher Negro house prices. Instead, he supports what he calls the 'customer preference hypothesis' which enables us to make sense of empirical observations of segregation characteristics. The key postulate is that whites have a greater aversion to living among Negroes than do other Negroes. Whites consequently are prepared to offer more for housing in white neighbourhoods than Negroes, and segregation is the result. On this view, segregation need not imply discrimination or higher Negro house prices. Indeed, an early analysis (Bailey, 1959) showed that house prices in the middle of Negro areas will be, in long-run equilibrium, lower than in the middle of white areas, and empirical data on Chicago supported this view.[24] In the border zone, on the other hand, house price differentials change. Prices on the non-white boundary tend to be higher than in the middle of the area, whereas prices on the white boundary tend to be lower than in the middle of the white area. This finding is consistent with the view that whites have an aversion to, but non-whites prefer, residential desegregation.

At first sight, the fact that Negro households spend a much higher proportion of their income on housing than whites may seem to contradict the above argument. This is not necessarily so. Firstly, the price elasticity of demand for housing probably exceeds unity. Secondly, substandard housing may be relatively more expensive than good quality housing for all races. The fact that a high proportion of Negroes live in poor housing is in large measure due to their lower incomes. Neither of these imply higher prices for Negroes of houses of a given quality.

Of course, these points do not mean that no discrimination exists. All they suggest is that there would be racial housing segregation even without discrimination. Discrimination in the housing market is difficult to document, but if any degree of

24. More recently, Muth (1969) found no evidence in Chicago that Negroes paid higher prices because of discrimination. In rented accommodation the race differential was very small but it was larger (of the order of 10 to 20 per cent) in single unit, owner-occupied dwellings.

discrimination, whether open or hidden, leads to non-whites being denied access to any part of the housing stock conditions are ripe for higher Negro house prices and overcrowding. The result is more certain in conditions of overall housing shortage[25] and/or when the rate of growth in non-white population is very high. In the United States in recent decades, large cities have been absorbing Negroes much faster than whites. On the other hand, Negroes have been heavily concentrated in the central core. Although this reinforces Negro housing demand, decentralization of white households into the suburbs has been an offsetting factor of some magnitude.

Much of the above analysis and the empirical generalizations stated relate to the United States. This reflects the high proportion of research in this field carried out in the United States, and this fact is scarcely surprising in view of the scale of the problem there. In the United Kingdom, the incidence of non-white households is much lower, and the black ghetto hardly exists. An analysis of 1961 Census data revealed that in London not one out of 4500 enumeration districts and in Birmingham not one out of 1400 had a majority of non-whites.[26] As in the United States, non-whites are concentrated in the older central cores of large cities. Four out of every five West Indians, for example, are to be found in six conurbations in England and Wales, most of them either in Greater London or in the West Midlands. Within the central cities, non-whites are the most segregated of any group. In the housing market, the most striking characteristic is that non-whites are heavily over-represented in furnished private rented accommodation but severely under-represented in local authority housing. In Greater London, for example, 40·8 per cent of West Indians live in the former (the figure for all households is 8·6 per cent) and only 4·0 per cent in the latter (21·6 per cent of all house-

25. In conditions of housing surplus, on the other hand, it will be very unprofitable for estate agents to support racial segregation.

26. In London the highest non-white share was 37 per cent and only forty-one EDs had more than 20 per cent; in Birmingham only 5 EDs had more than one-third of their populations black.

holds). These differences are not explained by the characteristics of the housing stock in which the immigrants live. Immigrants have become owner-occupiers in considerable numbers, though this has not prevented segregation from developing. Nor has it prevented housing conditions for immigrants being very poor. Furnished rented accommodation is notorious for overcrowding, while owner-occupiers have often been forced to sub-let to meet high mortgage repayments. In the London boroughs where West Indians are concentrated, 27 per cent of them live in conditions of severe overcrowding, that is more than 1·5 person per room (Haddon, 1970).

Racial housing segregation in Britain is obviously less marked than in the United States largely because the numbers involved are insufficient to create the housing market responses found in the States. Nevertheless, the segregation that is found tends to be racial in origin rather than a result of income, occupation or class. The clearest indication of this is the local authority sector where on grounds of income, occupation and class we would expect to find non-whites in strength. Instead, they are conspicuously absent. The reason for this is the largely unintentional discrimination rising out of council-housing eligibility rules. These rules include residential qualifications necessary in order to be accepted on the housing list and a points system weighted in favour of duration of residence or length of time on the list. In addition, many immigrants have been further disadvantaged because they have moved into bad housing areas with the longest lists.

In other segments of the housing market, particularly the private rented sector, access of non-whites has been restricted by more open discrimination, certainly before the Race Relations Act of 1968. As a result, immigrants have relied a great deal on personal contacts to find accommodation, often renting rooms from other immigrants, and this has tended to reinforce housing segregation. In the owner-occupied sector, especially in Inner London, immigrants are strongly represented. As in the United States, they are concentrated in the centrally located, old and often dilapidated housing which is difficult to sell to whites. Immigrants find it hard to gain access to the newer suburban housing estates. Confined to older houses, they find that only low mortgages can be raised on them. The houses they buy and their income status make them unappealing to the building societies, and they are often driven to the much more costly fringe institutions in the mortgage market. This is not fully offset, especially in tight credit conditions, by the willingness of local authorities, especially the Greater London Council, to grant them mortgages.

In the context of urban spatial structure, current trends show that, in a highly urbanized society with a sizeable proportion of non-whites, the non-whites tend to occupy the central cores of cities while the whites concentrate in the surrounding suburbs. Thus, in exploring the spatial structure of cities it is insufficient to explain this structure in terms of broad categories of land use. Residential land use has to be disaggregated not only by income groups as in Hoyt's radial sector model (1939) but also by race.

Racial segregation

Location

3 Urban Growth

Introduction

There is a great shortage of economic models of urban growth. One reason for this is the fact that urban economics is still in its infancy, and has not yet mastered how to adapt growth theory to the urban level of disaggregation or indeed faced up to the question of whether such an adaptation is possible. There are other explanations of this laggardly development. The complexity of the urban growth process, the diversity of urbanization experience particularly between countries at different levels of development, the recognition that the city is a social and cultural as well as an economic phenomenon, and the dearth of detailed empirical studies on urban growth from which meaningful and testable generalizations might be drawn: these are some of the obvious points.

A special problem facing the urban economist is that he usually lacks a satisfactory measure of urban growth. Growth in the national economy is invariably measured in output or income terms. However data of this kind are not available for cities as there are no urban social accounts, except in very rare circumstances, apart from the revenue and expenditure accounts of local authorities. In consequence, we tend to rely very heavily on demographic (including migration and employment) data, and associate urban growth with an increase in a city's population. Thus, even if there were indisputable evidence of a rise in total city output, some people might deny that urban growth was taking place with a declining population. Although the economist would normally regard population as a very poor proxy for an index of growth, it is widely used in the urban growth context. Although this wide use probably reflects the absence of any better indicator, some researchers have taken a more positive view: Lampard (1963) argues that 'the demographic approach appears to offer at once the least ambiguity and the most promise from the standpoint of observation and measurement'.

The emphasis in urban growth literature on increases in population rather than on rising *per capita* income means that there is a greater danger of a divergence between growth and welfare criteria. Thus, a city's growth, defined in population-change terms, need not imply an increase in the welfare of its citizens. In fact, in large cities there is some evidence that urban growth in the sense of an expanding population especially via migration brings about a fall in welfare. This is because of diseconomies of scale associated with the environment, pressure on the housing stock, rising living costs and excess demand on social overhead capital and welfare services. However, since growth in the national economy usually involves an increase in welfare, and urban growth is a major manifestation of national growth, we obtain the paradox that urban growth may mean an improvement in welfare *only* for those living outside the boundaries of the growing cities.

Leaving aside the interesting work by urban sociologists and ecologists, there are few *economic* models of urban growth. Of those that exist, one or two have been borrowed from other disciplines. All are fairly crude and elementary given the underdeveloped state of urban economics and the sparsity of statistical growth data on cities. None have a monopoly of truth, and all suffer from weaknesses. Choice among the theories available depends upon subjective judgement about which determinants are important, whether the theory can be expressed in terms of quantifiable variables, and upon the results of empirical tests.

Despite the parlous state of urban growth theory, understanding how and why cities grow is important both for its own sake and because of possible planning implications. Of course, market forces are no longer the sole determinants of city growth. The main reason for understanding why cities have grown in the past is *not* to predict their future growth, since planning decisions are capable of controlling many aspects of city development. But appreciation of the economic determinants of the urban growth process will help planners to make more efficient decisions and to help shape city growth. Although planners attempt to control population levels in the largest cities, they still desire to maximize income growth there. Moreover, there are many smaller cities and towns which are encouraged to expand, not to mention New Towns and growth points in which planners have actively had to foster economic development.

There is a body of analysis in the literature which is often discussed under the heading of 'urban growth' but which has little to do with the determinants and sources of urban growth. This type of analysis (of which Bourne (1969) and the models discussed in Lowry (1967) are fairly typical examples) tends to assume that the urban economy is growing, and then proceeds to explore the repercussions of growth on the spatial structure of the city.[1] Work in this field is concerned with such questions as the conversion of land from one use to another as a consequence of urban growth, the changing structure and functions of different parts of the city – especially the CBD – which are necessitated by urban development, and the changes in social and economic organisation, as implied in the work of ecologists (Schnore, 1965, for example). There is no doubt about the importance of analysis of this kind. It explicitly considers the variable space which is very desirable when our concern is with bounded urban areas, and it highlights the physical planning implications of growth and development. But it does not tell us why the city grows nor does it throw any light on the variations in city growth rates. For this reason I prefer to make an analytical distinction between the dynamics of spatial structure and the theory of urban growth.

1. This branch of urban analysis has already been examined in ch. 2 above, pp. 64–72.

Central place and urban base theory

The only economic theories of urban growth which have received widespread attention, if not acceptance, are central place analysis and urban base theory. Although they are suggestive in that each emphasises *one* possible key determinant of a city's growth, neither of them is satisfactory. They are based on concepts borrowed from disciplines other than economics, geography and planning respectively; they are in many respects crude and oversimplified; and while they may help to explain the development of some cities in certain phases of their growth, they lack generality.

According to the central place theory, the city grows as a result of supplying goods and services to the surrounding region. In other words, a city's growth is a function of its hinterland population (and income level). The main feature of this approach, the stress on links between city and region, is also its most serious limitation especially in highly urbanized economies. Firstly, cities grow for reasons other than servicing the hinterland, and large cities do not necessarily specialize in goods with broad market areas as central place theory claims. For instance, the process of city growth generates internal needs (for example car parking facilities, urban welfare agencies), and functions are transferred from households and firms to specialized service units. Secondly, central place analysis exaggerates the role of business and service activities. Manufacturing and transport are typical non-central-place activities, especially in a small country such as Britain where manufacturing firms tend to serve national rather than regional markets. Neither the growth of satellite centres (industrial estates, for example) nor suburban development fit easily into the central place framework. Thirdly, cities grow to a considerable extent by attracting resources (e.g. labour and capital) from outside. The inflow of migrants cannot be explained solely, or even primarily, in terms of the supply of central goods and services.

On the other hand, there is no doubt that central place concepts have some role in explaining urban development historically. Williamson and Swanson (1966) demonstrated that positive hinterland effects were important factors in the growth of nineteenth century cities in the north-east of the United States, though the impact of these effects diminished over time. Similarly, Higgs (1969), with regard to the growth of cities in the mid-West in the period 1870–1900, found support for the hypothesis that the greater the growth rate of population density in its trading area, the greater is the growth rate of the city, and showed that this factor was much more important than either industrialization or nodality. Even in modern times, there is some evidence that the hinterland effect influences the rate of in-migration to and growth of cities, as shown in von Boventer's study (1969) of postwar German urban development. Moreover, the concept of threshold market size, so critical to central place theory can contribute to our understanding of urban growth. Thus, Pred (1966) points out that certain regionally-oriented activities will not appear until a threshold size is reached, and argues that Löschian market area analysis, the manufacturing counterpart to central place services, implies that larger cities will have the greatest variety of manufacturing functions, a hypothesis tested by Tinbergen (1961) and by Bos (1965). This throws up the possible growth hypothesis that the rate of development in a city is functionally related to the diversification of its manufacturing sector. I emphasize this point not because tests of this hypothesis are likely to be fruitful but rather to illustrate that the inferences drawn from central place theory notions are not necessarily as restrictive as they might first appear. Finally, central place analysis has the advantage that it is a 'general' theory in this sense: it can explain the evolution of the urban hierarchy as well as the growth of the individual city.

In central place models the main source of city growth is the demand for goods and services in its hinterland; in urban base theory the source is demand from anywhere outside the boundaries of the urban centre. Also, urban base theory explicitly recognizes the existence of service industries that cater for no one but central city residents, but these industries are regarded as being 'dependent' on progress in the export sector. According to base theory a city grows as a result of specialization in exports, and its key tenet is, in the words of Pfouts (1958, p. 242), 'that exporting activity is the source and wellspring of urban economic growth.' Thus, in base models, the urban economy is treated as an endogenous system with exports as the sole exogenous determinant; investment is always induced. Like many monocausal explanations, this theory contains grains, but only grains, of truth. Its weaknesses are serious. The base ratio (the ratio of the size of the base to total economic activity) is a poor predictor of urban growth, particularly because the base ratio itself is inversely related to urban scale. Green (1966), for instance, found a significant relationship between city growth and the percentage of employment in local-market-oriented industries (for which he used tertiary employment as a proxy), and he put this down primarily to import substitution with an expanding local market.

Of course, forecasting demand for a city's current mix of export industries is a factor of some significance in its future growth. However, overemphasis on exports is dangerous. Urban investment (which may be local) can be autonomous, an exogenous source of growth additional to exports. The urban base protagonists would argue that if we seek the origin of the resources now available for investment we would trace it back to the export sector. The trouble with this argument is that one might then inquire about the preconditions for a thriving export sector, and this line of inquiry might lead straight to a conclusion, first pointed out by Blumenfeld (1955), that fast growth in cities depends not on the base sector itself but on the efficiency of the local service industries, since this determines how successfully the city can compete for mobile exporting firms, population and capital. In this sense a case could be made for turning base theory on its head, and making the export sector 'dependent' upon services. This would be going too far, but it does suggest that the attempt to establish a long-run causal sequence from either exports to services or vice versa is not very meaningful. It is more precise to stress the interdependence between base and service activities, and from this viewpoint urban base theory is much too oversimplified. It is true that some of the major defects of the theory can be obviated. For example, its excessive aggregation can be broken down by dividing exports into several sectors, as in the differential multiplier approach of Weiss and Gooding (1968). Nevertheless, the theoretical objections remain. Moreover, there are practical problems in measuring the base (for example delimitation of the urban area, classification of activities into basic and non-basic categories, reliance upon proxy measures of output) and these make even the urban base model difficult to test.

A location theory model of urban growth

Czamanski (1964) has developed a simple urban growth model which, while in some senses a derivative of urban base theory, contains a number of improvements and independent features. It links urban growth and industrial location theory by making the attraction of job-creating investments the chief determinant of the city's expansion and by arguing that the capacity to attract depends upon relative locational advantages and disadvantages. These location factors are not only market potential and the availability of least cost sites, but also external economies, socio-cultural amenities and other economies of urbanization. Czamanski's model is economical in information requirements; population is used as an index of city size, and employment as a proxy for economic activity. The urban economy is sectored into three divisions: geographically-oriented industries (E_g), complementary industries (E_c) and urban-oriented industries (E_u). Geographically-oriented industries are the mobile economic activities that can be attracted to a city by favourable locational and environmental factors. Complementary industries are industries for which the main locational determinant is the presence of other industries. They are usually small scale industries, and if input–output interrelationships were available it would normally show that firms in complementary industries sell their output to a limited number of enterprises in the same city. Urban-oriented industries, on the other hand, are industries which develop because of the very existence of the city; in small population centres such industries will be absent.

The model can be summarized in four equations:

$$P = a_1 + b_1 E \tag{1}$$

$$E = E_g + E_c + E_u, \tag{2}$$

$$E_c = a_2 + b_2 E_g, \tag{3}$$

$$E_u = a_3 + b_3 P, \tag{4}$$

where P is the population and E is employment, the as are constants and the bs regression coefficients. Thus, complementary industries are dependent upon geographically-oriented industries, while the size of the urban-oriented sector is a function of scale of city as denoted by the level of population. Via algebraic substitution, the solution of the above system is:

$$P = \frac{a_1 + b_1 (a_2 + a_3)}{1 - b_1 b_3} + \frac{b_1 (1 - b_2)}{1 - b_1 b_3} E_g. \tag{5}$$

Thus, city size can be expressed as a function of employment in geographically-oriented industry, which in turn depends upon how much mobile job-creating investment can be attracted to the city. The investment decisions of already present firms in the geographically-oriented sector and the location decisions of mobile firms become the key factor in urban growth.

Of course, as Czamanski himself accepts, this is a growth model in a somewhat restricted sense. It relates total population to aggregate employment in a particular sector, whereas in order to predict urban growth we need to relate ΔP to ΔE_g. To apply the model incrementally we require time-series data, and these are very scarce for individual cities. Moreover, better results can be obtained by sub-dividing the cities into a number of separate size-classes, particularly since the classification of industries may alter with variations in city size. Finally, the parameters derived from empirical observation are assumed stable. This means that the model throws no light on the time path traced by urban growth or on possible shifts in the parameters over time.

Scale and urban growth

A large number of urban analysts have, explicitly or implicitly, taken the view that city size is the main determinant of the rate of urban growth. This simple statement has been expressed in many different forms. Some argue, for instance, that economies of scale, agglomeration economies and indivisibilities favour the large city so much that big cities grow faster than small ones and that this tendency operates without limit to city size. Faced with empirical evidence of deceleration in growth or even absolute decentralization in large metropolises, the hypothesis is then modified. One modification is to draw attention to increasing pressure exerted by scale diseconomies beyond a certain (large) scale, and this raises the question of whether there might be an optimal city size. Another qualification is to argue that decentralization is the result of planning controls and regional policy measures, but that the faster growth of large cities would still be evident in a market environment. Other observers have focused their attention on the lower end of the urban size hierarchy. Pred (1966) and Thompson (1965) have stressed the importance of a minimum threshold limit. Urban growth is difficult until this threshold has been crossed, but then the growth rate accelerates and becomes self-generating; once across the threshold, the city will never contract back over it (the *urban size ratchet*).

The many variants of the scale hypothesis raise nagging doubts about its operational value. Even if there were an identifiable relationship between scale and growth rates, with or without an optimum city size or a lower threshold, it is probable that this relationship would vary over time, between regions and countries, and according to socio-economic and institutional environments. The generalized function

$$\dot{g} = f(P)$$

(where $\dot{g}$ is the growth rate, however measured, and P is the city population, used as an index of city size) is not very helpful unless we can specify the properties of the function more precisely. Williamson and Swanson (1966) tested on nineteenth century data the proposition that the urban growth function might have an inverted U-shape taking the form

$$\dot{g} = a + b_1 P - b_2 P^2$$

where the P^2 term could take account of possible scale diseconomies. Support for the scale hypothesis requires $b_1 > 0$ and $b_2 \leq 0$. If b_2 differs from zero, an optimal city size exists where

$$\frac{d\dot{g}}{dP} = b_1 + 2b_2 P = 0.$$

Their tests on cities in the American north-east between 1820 and 1870 rejected the scale hypothesis, because the coefficients failed to pass significant tests. A small consolation for the scale theory adherent was that the signs were always correct and the values of the parameters such that the optimum city size increased over time.

Apart from the likelihood that scale theories either fail empirical tests or lack generality because they apply only in a particular case, the main objection to them might be that they express only an empirically derived relationship and have no theoretical basis. This argument is hardly tenable in the sense that there are good theoretical reasons why size should promote growth potential. However, it may be difficult to evaluate the relative importance of the factors concerned, especially since many of them cannot easily be translated into quantifiable variables.

A number of reasons have been suggested why large cities should enjoy faster growth rates. Kuznets (1964) pointed to large scale economies in the use of social overhead capital and to the size of the local market in large urban centres. Lampard

(1955) emphasized advantages on the input side: the advantages of access to a metropolitan labour pool and to developed capital markets. Scale permits greater specialization and hence improved efficiency.

Another factor favouring large cities stems from the marked tendency for the share of external trade in total urban activity to be inversely related to city size. The larger a city, the more self-contained it will be. Since this will save transport costs to and from other areas, a large city should, *ceteris paribus*, be a more efficient unit.

Pred (1966) stressed the benefits of 'initial advantage'. Existing locations are characterized by a great deal of inertia, and advantages pile up over time; furthermore, existing locations exert considerable influence on subsequent plant location decisions, so that once concentration is established it develops a self-perpetuating momentum. This type of economy is primarily a locational advantage resulting in most cases from the agglomeration of several firms within an industry. These *localization economies* have to be distinguished from *urbanization economies*, the external economies generated by large urban units. The latter exercise a locational pull over and above the attraction of the urban market. They include economies of scale in the provision of urban government services, in private business services, and in social, cultural and leisure facilities. Some of these can be provided more efficiently on a large scale; others can be supplied *only* above a threshold urban size because they need a large market area to support them. These external economies often exert an influence not simply by cost reductions in production but, more dynamically, by attracting migrants, capital, managers and other decision-makers, highly skilled personnel including technologists and innovators. In this way, the growth potential of large urban centres is enhanced. They remain, or become, the leading centres of innovation, they benefit from professional and technical personnel of the highest calibre, and they have easy access to the most highly skilled labour pools. Ullman (1962) described this phenomenon of size attracting size as a mass gravity effect. If the locational attraction exerted by these external agglomeration economies increased functionally with size,[2] this would strongly reinforce the scale theory.

In assessing the impact of scale on urban growth, it is useful to make an analytical distinction between the effect of cost reductions on the one hand and productivity gains and technical advances associated with agglomeration economies on the other. In the first case, we assume a given level of technology and draw up a long-run average unit cost curve. Costs are defined to include the aggregate of production costs and the cost of municipal services, and city size (as measured by population) is represented on the horizontal axis. If the scale hypothesis holds, the cost curve will decline with increasing city size, and if an optimal city size exists the curve will assume the classical U-shape. In Williamson and Swanson's analysis (1966), the long-run average cost curve is the mirror image of their urban growth function, so that they in effect assume that the growth of the city is proportional to the reciprocal of its average cost (C). Thus,

$$\dot{g} = kC^{-1}$$

where k is a positive constant.

While it is possible to take account of technological improvements in this analysis, by downward shifts towards the right in the long-run cost curve, this is a very imperfect way of expressing the role of external and agglomeration economies. This is particularly because these economies manifest themselves more in market potential gains, higher incomes and social benefits than in reduced costs. Yet when we try to measure the impact of external economies we are faced with insuperable problems because 'there is almost no agreement on how external economies are defined', and therefore 'little hope of quantification' (Darwent, 1969). One attempt at measurement has been made by Marcus (1965). If the urban growth rate in a given industry is higher than the national growth rate

2. Pred (1966) makes this suggestion, and it is consistent with the argument advanced earlier in the book (see above p. 17).

weighted by the relative growth of population in the area he attributed the 'extra' growth to external economies. Thus, the external economy effect is measured by the difference between the actual growth rate in the city ($\dot{g}_c$) and the hypothetical growth rate ($\dot{g}_n \dot{P}_c/\dot{P}_n$) where c and n are subscripts for the city and the nation respectively and $\dot{P}$ is the rate of population growth. Interesting as this approach is, it is unsatisfactory. In particular, it is probably a much better measure of localization economies than of urbanization and agglomeration economies. In practice, it does little more than provide a variant of the 'differential shift' technique familiar to regional analysts.[3]

The urban growth function will turn downwards if diseconomies begin to overwhelm agglomeration economies in large cities. Such diseconomies might include pecuniary external diseconomies (such as rising costs, high wage levels and increasing public-service costs) and the presence of these might have a marked effect on the city's capacity to attract new growing industries. Although traffic congestion may have an adverse effect on growth, other environmental diseconomies such as pollution and blight, despite being perhaps the most serious diseconomies of urban scale from a social point of view, are unlikely to inhibit growth to any great extent unless pricing policies are adopted to make firms pay for social costs. There may also be bottlenecks or thresholds in infrastructure and urban development costs which slow down growth pending an increase in the rate of public investment, but these will occur in steps along the growth path and are not solely confined to large urban centres.

Another reason for a slowing down of growth rates in large cities may be that positive action is taken to prevent further urban expansion by planners. Planned decentralization can be very effective especially in a planned economy, as the experience of the Soviet Union shows for example. Even in mixed economies, such as France and the United Kingdom, attempts to decentralize economic activities, especially office establish-

3. For examples of this see Perloff, Dunn, Lampard and Muth (1960) and Stilwell (1969).

ments, from the metropolises have met with varying degrees of success. Space constraints imposed by the built environment, however, are unlikely to restrain urban growth to a significant degree. For one thing, growth usually takes place first and the necessary adjustments in spatial structure follow only gradually. Secondly, whereas *a priori* one might expect growth in very large cities to be slowed down by congestion of structures, this need not happen. In older cities, the redevelopment of large central areas often permits much more growth to be accommodated. Moreover, many cities are not short of open land at their boundaries, and paradoxically an increase in city size is often associated with a fall in average densities.

The scale hypothesis has a certain attraction as a theory of urban growth because of its simplicity and, in some variants, elegance. It stands or falls, however, by how it bears up to empirical tests. Furthermore, even if supported empirically, the theoretical foundations of the hypothesis would require much closer specification. Headway in this direction probably demands a deeper understanding of the external economies of agglomeration and how these might be measured.

Empirical evidence on the scale hypothesis is scanty, inadequate and conflicting. To point to a trend increase in average city size is irrelevant, of course, since the average city size is bound to increase even if every city grows at a constant and equal rate. The scarcity of urban output data makes it necessary in most cases to measure urban growth with the aid of a proxy such as population or employment. Available evidence does not always point in the same direction. In the United States, the large cities of more than two million population have, *taken as a whole*, increased their populations in recent decades more slowly than in smaller cities, but when the size classes are disaggregated we find that the West Coast metropolises expanded much faster than the national average. In the United Kingdom, on the other hand, the conurbations have grown much more slowly than smaller urban areas. This raises a problem: since it is clear that planning and regional policy decisions can have a substantial influence on rates of urban growth, the scale hypothesis really needs to be tested in a market-oriented environment. This is why historical tests of the kind carried out by Williamson and Swanson are so important. On the other hand, it might be argued that diseconomies of scale, if they exist at all, are characteristic of twentieth century cities, and if this is the case more recent data are required. Moreover, virtually none of the empirical studies have attempted to specify and calibrate the urban growth functions but have been limited to comparing the rates of (population) growth in cities by size class alone. Finally, in most countries we are likely to find both slow growth and rapid expansion within small, medium and large cities alike, and until we know *why* size may be important it is almost impossible to separate out the influence of the scale variable from other determinants of the rate of urban growth.

Supply oriented urban growth models

Most of the accepted theories of urban growth (export base, central place and input–output) are demand oriented. Very rarely is the supply side of urban growth given any emphasis.[4] This bias is rather odd. In the first place, analysis of growth in national economies has concentrated in recent years on supply approaches, particularly neoclassical models. Secondly, whereas demand models are appropriate for comparative statistics analysis where we can identify a fairly clear relationship between a change in, say, export sales and a change in urban income, they are not so relevant in the long run. In the short run it is reasonable to think of urban-regional flows in terms of commodity trade; in the long run, however, a city's capacity for growth is determined less by export sales than by the in-migration of labour and inflows of capital. Factor flows are at the heart of the growth process in open economies such as the city, and this suggests looking at growth from the input (that is, supply) side.

4. For an exception see Winger (1969). It is a pity that Winger's analysis comes to a sharp halt just as he has begun to indicate the main elements of a supply model.

Thirdly, demand models may have been more relevant to explanations of urban growth in the nineteenth century when cities were more highly specialized, but the livelihood of that complex phenomenon – the modern metropolis – is not so closely tied to shifts in demand in a few key industries. Given that, with changes in transport technology and the reduced reliance on raw materials and natural resources in location, industry is much more mobile than it used to be, a city's growth potential depends upon whether it contains or can attract the resources (highly skilled manpower, managerial talent, research and development facilities, capital market access, specialized business services, etc.) that are capable of luring the new or growing footloose firm. Urban growth depends according to this view on the city's relative locational advantages which in the context of modern location theory are based on the supply of human resources and specialist services offered.

Finally, supply models should be at least as satisfying conceptually as demand models since in many cases they can be derived simply by inverting the model's basic assumptions. Thus, export base theory assumes that the demand for labour is completely inelastic while the supply of labour function is perfectly elastic. Thus, the source of growth is exogenous change in export demand. A supply-oriented model, on the other hand, treats the city's demand for labour as highly elastic, its labour supply as inelastic and the supply of labour as exogenous.[5] In criticising the demand approach, we must be careful not to enshrine supply orientated models in its place. A more satisfactory methodology would be to emphasize their mutual interdependence, and with regard to migration in particular it is perhaps significant that recent work by Muth (1968b) and Lowry (1966) has drawn attention to the need for a simultaneous equation approach.

5. Of course, by introducing many more variables into the system it is possible to explain increases in the supply of labour endogenously. See the model of migration described below (pp. 101–2).

A verbal description of a supply-oriented urban growth model presents no difficulty. The growth potential of a city depends upon its ability to create and attract from outside the productive resources needed for growth as well as on its ability to produce the goods and services in demand in regional, national and international markets. The growth of the city, as of the region or nation, is determined by its rate of population growth, its rate of capital investment and its rate of technological progress, widely interpreted. However, there are limits on the city's capacity to expand its stock of resources *internally*: the rate of natural increase in city population, the capital accumulation of local firms, and the propensity of local managers and innovators to raise productivity. Internally-generated expansion is usually insufficient to enable cities to experience fast growth rates. To grow fast, a city must obtain productive factors from outside, and act as a magnet for migrants, outside capital, non-local managerial talent and skilled technical personnel, and innovation. Large cities are usually much better fitted for this task than small urban centres. Their developed labour markets and wider job opportunities are more attractive to the migrant, especially the long-distance migrant. Large cities are looked on with great favour by outside investors particularly in consumer-goods industries and services where access to a large potential market reduces risks. The metropolises often have the variety of amenities, cultural and leisure facilities necessary to attract executives, scientists and members of the professions from other cities and regions. They also tend to be the leading centres of innovation, partly because of the mutually reinforcing concentration of large firms, scientists and technologists and research institutes, partly because their cosmopolitan outlook (or in Webber's terminology (1964), a high degree of communication with non-place urban realms) makes them more likely to absorb new ideas and innovations from outside, especially from abroad. The strong tendency for managerial talent to be concentrated in large cities partly reflects the demand for executives in the metropolis, but is also affected by their preference for living and working in or near large cities because they offer the shopping, social, leisure and cultural amenities that the professional classes require. There is evidence (the pioneering work of Ullman (1958) for example) of massive localization of centres of decision-making, leading scientists and technologists, university and specialist libraries, research institutes, patent activity, and so on in large cities. For all these reasons growth in large cities will tend to be self-generating, particularly because these agglomeration economies – primarily external economies of scale – give the large city a great advantage in obtaining additional growth inputs from outside.[6] It should be noticed how much this analysis stresses the advantages of scale, and this emphasis is brought out even more clearly in the more formal analysis given below. This gives further indirect theoretical support to the scale hypothesis, and shows that apparently alternative theories are not necessarily incompatible.

In descending from the level of the national economy to that of the urban economy, we must take care to modify the explanatory growth models if appropriate to reflect the change in scale and environment. In urban growth theory it may be necessary to change some of the key assumptions and to add or delete variables. Consider, for example, the question of returns to scale. In neoclassical growth models of the national economy it is common to assume constant returns to scale. This makes it possible to retain perfect competition and to measure factor contributions to growth with the aid of classical distribution theory. In the fast-growing city, however, it is only reasonable to assume increasing returns to scale. Why? The importance of agglomeration economies in urban growth has already been emphasized. The second reason is rather

6. R. L. Meier (1963) is even more specific about the pre-requisites a city needs to attract the sources of growth. They include (i) immediate access to cultural amenities; (ii) adjacency to a major research-oriented university or hospital; (iii) nearness to large capital-intensive installations; (iv) a professional class suburban environment; (v) access to trunk transport routes; (vi) availability of cheap general purpose structures.

more complicated. The individual city cannot be considered in isolation from the system of cities which contains it. Within the system some cities must be growing at any one time. Since negative growth is unknown in a developed economy (even though growth rates may differ widely) and since such economies are urbanized, it follows that some cities must also grow. The cities in the system are in competition with each other, and a high growth rate in a city represents success in this competitive struggle. But what determines which cities in the system will grow? The answer is found in the ability of particular cities to attract resources from outside. The most probable explanation of why some cities can attract growth inputs is because they offer increasing returns to scale. It is true that a constant returns to scale assumption is possible in an initial disequilibrium situation in which some cities offer higher returns to factors than others, but once factor mobility has equalized factor returns between cities, then each city would grow at the rate determined by its natural increase of population and its internal rates of capital accumulation and technical progress. But city growth rate variations are much wider than can be accounted for by internal expansion. Urban growth differentials resulting from interurban competition imply increasing returns to scale in rapidly growing cities.[7]

The other major difference between urban and national growth is that a city's growth rate is subject to certain constraints which are not operative in the national (or even the regional) economy. The most important of these constraints are as follows:

1. *Space constraints*. This needs to be taken into account in urban growth analysis. It has two components: the shortage

7. The observant reader will notice that this conclusion depends upon the assumption of at least constant returns to scale in the national economy. If constant returns to scale are assumed at the national level and if growth is concentrated on some rather than all cities, it follows from the above analysis that increasing returns should be assumed in growing cities. But if we assumed diminishing returns to scale in the national economy, the cities with above average growth rates may experience constant (or even slightly diminishing) returns.

of urban land and a density constraint. Land shortage can never hold up growth in the national economy, but it can affect the rate of expansion in an individual city. The density constraint may be either the limited capacity of existing physical structures or controls externally imposed by planners. The space limitation can be linked to an economic variable, the city's population level, if it is expressed as $P \leqslant dU$ where d is maximum density, and U is area of available urban land. Although this constraint is serious, its importance *in the long run* can be exaggerated. U is a variable which can be increased either by peripheral expansion or by filling in of open space and odd plots, while d is a variable that can be increased most easily by increasing the plot ratio.[8] I would expect space and land constraints to be an obstacle to urban growth in the short run, but they can be obviated in the long run.

2. *Rate of construction constraint.* A characteristic feature of urban growth is extension of the stock of physical structures (houses, shops, offices, roads, public buildings, etc.). A short-term increase in demand for the city's products will not require any change in the building stock, but inflows of labour and capital other than on a marginal scale certainly will. Therefore, the capacity of the construction industry (and how quickly this can be increased in response to the pressures of growth) places an upper limit on the urban growth rate.

3. *Labour market constraint.* The supply of labour depends upon the rate of natural increase, the net migration rate and variations in the labour participation rate. In this case too, however, there is an upper limit on the growth rate of labour related to the demand for labour in the urban labour market. This constraint can be expressed as $L_S \leqslant L_D$ where L is labour force and the subscripts refer to supply and demand. Regardless of the factors motivating migrants, for example high wage levels in cities, the rate of in-migration and any increase in the

8. A plot ratio of five to one means that all the site is covered by five storeys, or half the site by ten storeys, and so on.

overall labour participation rate will be constrained by the rate of growth in employment. Since the latter will be determined by the rate of growth in demand for the city's industries and services, the labour market constraint is important because it illustrates the interdependence of demand and supply in urban growth.

4. *Planning constraint.* Urban physical planners have the peculiar distinction that, in contrast to regional and national policy-makers, they can hold up growth completely.[9] This can result from not allowing land to be released for development, land use controls or density standards (these link up with (1) above). In some cases, such controls will be justified by the need to maintain urban design and planning standards and to present deterioration in the environment as a consequence of growth. In other cases, however, they may result from the value judgements of planners as to whether or not growth is desirable. That planners should be willing to permit growth, and indeed that they should take the decisions which promote and stimulate it, is an important pre-condition of urban growth.

To sum up the above analysis the crucial determinants of city growth would seem to be: the ability to attract resources from outside its boundaries, the availability and intensity-of-use of space, and the attitude of planners to growth.[10] Of these three factors, the latter two are better treated as constraints on, rather than contributions to, growth. We are thus left with the 'city as a magnet' thesis as the main component of the urban growth model. The verbalized statement of the supply analysis outlined above can be translated into more formal terms by taking the neoclassical growth equation:

$$y = al + bk + r \tag{6}$$

9. Some restrictions are possible at the regional level, for example negative controls in prosperous regions, but are hardly feasible at the national level in a mixed economy other than via the effects of monetary and fiscal policy.

10. The labour market and rate of construction constraints do not determine the rate of urban growth, but merely its upper limits.

where y, l, k and r are the growth rates of output, labour, capital and technical progress (or the 'residual') respectively, and where in a national growth model, assuming constant returns, $a + b = 1$. Transforming this into an urban context, we drop the constant returns to scale assumption and treat a and b as parametric variables where $(a + b) \gtreqless 1$ from city to city. The main determinant of the rate of capital accumulation (both within the city and from outside as capital inflows) will be the existence or otherwise of increasing returns in the city's industries which are primarily due to localization and urbanization economies. These are closely related to city size, so that we can express the rate of growth in capital as an increasing function of city size (as measured by population):

$$k \text{ is } fP^\alpha \qquad \alpha > 1, \tag{7}$$

where f is a constant.

Similarly, the rate of productivity growth, technical advances and other components in the residual will be determined by the agglomeration economies found within the city. Thus,

$$r = gP^\beta \qquad \beta > 1, \tag{8}$$

where g is a constant. Substituting (7) and (8) into (6) we obtain

$$y = al + bfP^\alpha + gP^\beta. \tag{9}$$

In the special, but not necessarily unusual, case where α equals β, the growth equation collapses to

$$y = al + (bf + g)P^\alpha. \tag{10}$$

This form not only simplifies empirical testing, it may also be justifiable theoretically if technical progress is 'embodied' in capital accumulation.

The urban growth rate can accordingly be expressed in terms of two major independent variables, the rate of growth of labour and city size. The model assumes that the rates of both capital stock growth and technical progress are determined by localization, urbanization and other agglomeration economies. Moreover, in a fast-growing city the joint value of the parametric variables $(a + b)$ will be greater than 1, and may itself be an increasing function of P.

In the present state of knowledge, the analysis of the links between urban growth and external economies of scale cannot be taken much further than the general comments already mentioned. However, the other major independent variable, the rate of growth in the labour supply, can be analysed in a little more detail. This growth rate may be stated as

$$l = q(n + m) \tag{11}$$

where n equals the rate of natural increase, m equals the net migration rate (that is the number of net migrants divided by city population), and q equals 1 if the labour participation rate remains constant but may change in value to reflect variations in labour force participation. The rate of natural increase can be regarded as being exogenously determined. The migration rate can be influenced by a host of factors, and many models have been proposed at one time or another. Most of them, however, stress the importance of the size of the centre of destination. Von Boventer (1969) shows, for example, that city size has a marked influence on the inflow of migrants in cities within the 250,000 to 500,000 range. The size of the destination is also a key variable in gravity models of migration, possibly the most common type of interarea migration model in current use. Many observers emphasize the importance of rapid employment and income growth as factors inducing migration. Lowry (1966), for example, states that over time, net migration to a given city has a direct relationship to the growth of employment there, and an inverse relationship to the natural increase of the resident labour force. Using the rate of income growth as a proxy for employment growth, we can combine these ideas by adopting a linear regression model for determining the rate of migration,

$$m = x_1 y + x_2 P - x_3 n. \tag{12}[11]$$

In the case where q equals 1 (that is abstracting from variations

11. To simplify, we ignore the constant and error terms, x_0 and u.

in labour force participation) if we substitute equation **12** into **11** we may write:

$$l = x_1 y + x_2 P + (1-x)n. \tag{13}$$

As already pointed out, Muth (1968) and Lowry (1966) have put a great deal of stress on the feedback effects of growth on migration and of population (labour supply) expansion on growth. Thus, by inducing migration, a high urban growth rate boosts the rate of growth of labour supply, while expansion in the labour supply helps to raise the growth rate. Equations **10** and **13** considered together give us an interaction model of this kind. If we substitute **13** into **10** and solve for y, we obtain:

$$y = \frac{(1-x_3)an + P[ax_2 + (bf+g)^{\alpha-1}]}{1 - ax_1} \tag{14}$$

By adopting a migration model of the type implied in equation **12**, we are able to express the urban growth rate in terms of two basic variables, city size and the rate of natural increase. The migration flow no longer requires separate treatment since it can be described in terms of y, P and n.

4 Urban Transportation

Of all urban economic problems none has attracted as much attention as the urban transport sector. Articles in the learned journals, millions of pounds and dollars in the research institutes, conferences between traffic engineers, transport planners and town planners, billions of pounds and dollars of investments in public transit facilities – the expenditure of resources and effort has been immense. Despite this, many of the problems thrown up by urban transport are as far away from a solution as ever. Others can be solved, but the political will to implement the required measures is lacking. This chapter attempts to outline some of these problems and to examine a few of the proposed remedies. Needless to say, it offers no panaceas.

Apart from its specific focus – the movement of people and, to a lesser extent, of goods around cities – a discussion of urban transport illustrates some of the more general features of the urban economy rather well. Divergences between private and social costs, indivisibilities in urban investments, the potential conflict between individual preferences and planning requirements, the interrelatedness of everything in the city – these roots of recurrent dilemmas in analysis of the city crop up in what follows. Although urban transportation is, above all, a severely practical problem, resolution of some of the theoretical questions it poses should prise open doors to other locked-away secrets of urban economic theory.

The 'peak' problem

Although 'peaking' problems arise in many branches of public enterprise, they are found in a particularly acute form in urban transportation. Urban travel flows are much denser in morning and evening rush hours on weekdays than at other times, a fact that obviously reflects the dominance of travel to work in urban journeys. The load factor (that is the ratio of average load to peak load) can be as low as 33 per cent on an urban transport facility compared with, say, 75–80 per cent on an electric power transmission system (Kuhn, 1965). The flow of traffic during the morning peak in a city centre may be forty or fifty times as heavy as in the middle of the night. For many mass-transit facilities, 80 per cent of the traffic volume is concentrated in twenty hours of the week. Another aspect of 'peaking' in urban transport, of course, is that there is a concentration in space as well as in time, with the highest flows being found in the CBD, on radial roads or at limited capacity points in the network, such as the only bridge over a river.

The 'peaking' problem is insoluble. At best, the measures to deal with it are palliatives. One approach is to encourage transport modes with a good peak performance. This favours public transport, especially rail. Rail transit has the highest peak hour capacity, but unfortunately this is often accompanied by the lowest off-peak demands. But it is expensive and uneconomic to satisfy peak demand in this way, for additional public investment is likely to sharpen the peaks, reduce the load factor and raise operating costs (especially the per trip cost of the plant). Moreover, rail transit is very inflexible and it is difficult to adjust either the scale of service or, especially, its locational pattern. Where the costs are already 'sunk', the existence of a long-established urban rail network can be a tremendous boon; in Central London for example, more than three-fifths of the journeys during the morning peak are by rail. But it is difficult to make new systems pay. Even so, there have been many plans to cater for peak usage in schemes such as the Bay Area Rapid Transit District (BARTD) system for San Francisco or the Manchester Rapid Transit Study. It is clear that rail transit systems have a much higher capacity than other forms of transport, hence their appeal in highly concentrated population centres. Moreover, they are probably cheaper to build than most *urban* motorways. Yet the peaking problem is not really solved with such systems, despite attempts to improve the load factor by, say, luring shoppers to rail transit.

The use of buses provides a compromise solution. These play an important role in peak hours in some provincial cities in Britain such as Birmingham, Leeds and Newcastle. They are more flexible and involve lower capital costs than rail, use urban space more efficiently than the car, and can do an effective job if combined with attempts to optimize the use of the road system, by creating separate lanes or other means of priority access or by measures to reduce congestion due to cars. The private car, on the other hand, is totally inadequate as a peak-service mode. It is a profligate consumer of urban space, its speed (in peak hours) is low, it is relatively unsafe, and its social costs (such as air pollution) are very high. Even more important, it is impossible to build central roads which could cope with peak travel demand by car alone. A computer simulation for Montreal in 1980 showed that it would be necessary to have fourteen to twenty-two lanes for every freeway link within six miles of the city centre. Nevertheless, the preference for private car travel is so strong that immense efforts are necessary to prevent continued growth in its use in peak hours.

One view is that congestion itself will choke off demand and induce some shift to other modes or encourage commuters to make other adjustments. There is something to be said for this. Lower income groups have more leisure and value it less than higher income groups. The latter have more discretionary control over their working hours and are often capable of devising ways of escaping road congestion costs. Thus, rationing by congestion is a form of progressive taxation scheme that places the major incidence of congestion costs on those groups most able to take corrective measures (Meyer, Kain and Wohl, 1965, p. 340). Price rationing, on the other hand, may hit at low-income workers who are unable to alter their time of travelling. But since the social costs of congestion (particularly time losses) may be very high, charging more to peak users may be a more appropriate remedy despite this danger of regressive effects. If price controls are adopted, they will be ineffective unless the peak fare differentials on public transport are accompanied by user charges on private cars which also differentiate between times of the day (Vickrey, 1965), and this requires much greater sophistication in methods of road pricing.

Other attempts to tackle the 'peaking' problem require us to tamper with the spatial and temporal organization and structure of the city, and hence may involve a trade-off between general economic efficiency and improved transport performance. Steps under this heading include considering the feasibility of introducing staggered working hours and the possibilities of reducing the need for face-to-face contact between different departments of an establishment's labour force or between businessman and client by replacing the physical movement of people with communication by telephone or teletransmission of data. A more long-term strategy in the same direction is to intervene via the physical planning mechanism to rearrange urban land use patterns, particularly to decentralize workplaces, so as to reduce urban transport peaks. The dispersion of activities from the centre reduces the spatial peaks on a few corridors by replacing them with more homogeneous, less dense and criss-crossing trip densities. The coordination of such planning measures with urban transport investment is, however, a critical factor, since the main impact of decentralization is to increase the comparative advantage of the private car.

Modal choice

There are two viewpoints one may take when choosing the best mode, that of the user of urban transport and that of the transport planner. These choices do not necessarily yield identical results. The reason for this possible, even likely, divergence is the presence of externalities. The consumer in selecting his mode of travel pays attention only to his private costs and benefits. These could differ substantially from social costs and benefits. This divergence is particularly acute in the case of the motor car. Congestion, air pollution, noise, accidents and absorption of urban space are major social costs, while the clearest external benefit, the high employment and income multiplier effect of car production and vehicle service, is unlikely to enter into the transport planner's calculus. It is, of course, possible for private and social costs to be brought closer together by user charges and other pricing policies. Even then, however, there is no guarantee that the individual user will select the mode that is most consistent with economic efficiency. He may fail to appreciate the full costs involved in his choice; for example, if he chooses to travel by car he may underestimate depreciation or ignore the valuation of his own travel time. Possession and use of his own personal form of transport may confer 'psychic income' benefits to which it is impossible to assign a monetary value. In such circumstances it may be very difficult indeed to persuade the commuter to travel by public transport.

There are several variables which could influence the individual's modal choice. Quarmby (1967) suggested the following variables: relative journey time, amount of time spent walking or waiting for transport, cost, and the availability of parking space. Reynolds (1966) listed a rather different set of factors: car ownership (which depends primarily upon income and residential density), the frequency and convenience of public transport as measured by average journey time per mile, congestion and lack of parking space. Many of these variables are intercorrelated with others such as population density and size of the urban population, which by affecting the level of public transport services offered constrain the choice facing the individual. Schnore (1962) argued that three variables, population size (which determines the scale of the market), population density (which determines the economy of operation) and the age of urban area (early developed cities have more public transit facilities since they were mainly built prior to the car explosion) accounted for two-thirds of the variance among cities in the extent to which public transport was used for commuting to work, and that of these three variables, age was the most important. Size of urban area nevertheless is of some significance. Oi and Shuldiner (1962) found some years ago that expenditure on cars increased relatively with decreasing city size, while in both Britain and the United States there is a marked tendency for the proportion of commuters travelling by mass transportation to be higher the larger the city (see the tables reprinted in Hall, 1969). This does not of course mean that the preferences of commuters in large cities are very different from those in smaller centres, but merely reflects the fact that the choices facing transport users vary according to city size.

Since there is strong evidence of a very high income elasticity of demand for private car transportation services and a low elasticity for public transport services, there is some tendency as incomes rise over time for custom to shift away from mass transit.[1] Kain (1969), for instance, has shown that increases in service frequency have little effect on public transport demand. Reductions in fares on public transport have little impact on numbers of passengers, and Moses and Williamson (1963) argued that even free public transport would attract less than one-third of urban car commuters.

Why do consumers of transport services react in this way? In the first place, the choice may be entirely rational even in cost terms, provided that travel time is valued highly. Given this assumption, car transport may be cheaper estimated on a door-to-door basis than alternative modes up to a commuting distance of fifteen miles. Secondly, the car is very flexible and may offer advantages to commuters which outweigh any cost differential. Privacy, door-to-door travel, no stops, no need to change modes, comfort, these benefits may be highly prized if the commuter does not mind the burden of driving and if

1. Moreover, both car ownership and income (as well as the members of the household in question who are working) have an impact on the total demand for transport services by increasing the number of journeys made.

either he has two cars or his car is not needed during the day at home.

Such behaviour by urban transport users presents serious problems to the transportation planner in many cities. Only if the city is strongly decentralized with widely diffused origins and destinations will the motor car be the most efficient means of transport.[2] Cities of this kind are still very atypical. Rail will be the best mode only if urban population densities are very high and/or long journeys to work from densely populated suburbs are dominant among urban traffic flows. In most other cases, especially when *new* investments have to be made, the bus will be the most efficient mode provided it is given appropriate operating conditions. This means having a separate right of way (unless general-use urban freeways have no congestion problems) and automatic surveillance, monitoring and central control so that the urban transport network operates as a coordinated system. A bus system is, especially in medium size cities, more than fully competitive with rail. Its peak hour speeds are satisfactory if congestion is overcome, partly because buses can pick up passengers nearer their point of origin partly because their small size means fewer stops for a full load. Its capital costs are lower. It is a very flexible system which can easily adjust to changes in the location of activities and in the level of demand. In towns below a certain size, however, it is difficult to make a comprehensive bus service 'pay' in financial accounting terms. The growth in car ownership has made life hard for any public transport system, depriving it of passengers thereby inducing the syndrome of 'fewer passengers – higher fares and poorer services – even fewer passengers'. Transit movement has been slowed down through congestion; and a pattern of low density centrifugal residential development has been promoted which is difficult to serve by public transport. In these circumstances, the solution may be public subsidies since an efficient bus system (including high frequency service, 'charter' buses between residential areas

2. The car will also be the most efficient mode in small population centres where the total traffic volume is very low.

and workplaces, and so on) may yield a much greater excess of social benefits over social costs than building flyovers, creating parking spaces and all the other investment requirements necessary to accommodate the private car (see the study of Stevenage by Lichfield, 1970b).

The collection and delivery problems

The above discussion of modal choice has been artificial in that it has compared one *single* mode with another. It is widely recognized that raising efficiency in urban transport very often necessitates adopting the best features of two or more modes. This is very much related to the collection and delivery problem. Collection is a problem because of the low density patterns prominent in suburban residential development, while the delivery problem has been aggravated, firstly by changes in scale and distribution of activities in the CBD (most of which have tended to lengthen the journey from the terminal to the workplace), and secondly, by the dispersal of workplaces. The aggravation of these problems has accentuated the difficulties of public transport. If minimization of travel time is important to commuters, the goal is to make total origin-to-destination time competitive with that achieved by the door-to-door service of the private car (assuming that parking facilities are available at the workplace). Public transport vehicles have two serious handicaps: they have to stop and start to take on (and let off) passengers, and passengers have to get to the stops. The delivery question can arise, however, with both public and private transport since car parks may be as far away from work as bus or rail terminals.

These problems can in some cases be tackled by the public sector. For instance, buses may be provided from residential suburbs to rail stations where the commuters change modes for a faster journey to work. Passenger conveyor belts for distributing people from public transport terminals can have quite a high capacity (a belt forty-two inches wide for instance can carry three times as many people per hour as a main road). Their main drawback at present is their speed; travelling at about two miles per hour in order to allow people to jump on and off easily means that they are practicable only for short distances. Mainline train and central underground is a common solution in many cities. Private individuals may also devise their own solutions. Public transport and walking is the most common combination of modes, while 'park'n ride' where the commuter drives his car from home to a railway station where he leaves it or 'kiss'n ride' where he arranges for his wife to drive him to and pick him up from the station are also widely adopted. Attention to collection and delivery is essential for an efficient urban transport system, and emphasizes just how misleading speaking in terms of the single most efficient mode can be. The design of fast and effective transit feeder systems is just as important as improving long-distance mass transit commuter lines, but with the former as much as with the latter, high costs require high capacity and high average rates of utilization.

Technical change

Faced with the virtually insoluble urban transport dilemma, there is a great temptation to hope for some miraculous revolution wrought by technological change. This is likely to be a false hope. There are some bright ideas, already technically feasible or on the verge of being so. But they are often very costly to implement. Moreover, most of the advances help to make public transport more competitive with the private car and have an uphill struggle to hold in check the strong trend in favour of the car. It is also probable that the more consequential developments will affect intercity and international transport rather than urban transportation itself. For example, the marked acceleration now possible in the speed of long-distance passenger trains and the future scope for STOL (Short Take Off and Landing) aircraft as a passenger mode.

There are many technical possibilities, some of which are not yet operationally feasible, others which have already been introduced on an experimental scale in some parts of the world. These include the use of small electrically-powered cars for central city use, possibly on automatic freeways on which the cars can be coupled and uncoupled (for automatic control and to permit easy storage in the CBD); a similar high speed automatic track for public transport vehicles; automation of the flow of traffic; computer controlled bus-taxi system permitting individual dialling; passenger conveyor belt systems for distribution from public transit in the city centre; techniques for scanning passing vehicles (electronic methods including small code-signal transmitters, photoelectric equipment, and radar scanners); elevated monorails which have the serious disadvantage that they are not suitable for residential or commercial areas. Some of these developments are appropriate in particular circumstances for certain cities; none is a universal solution.

Indeed, it might be argued that the most beneficial results may be obtained by the simplest of innovations. Meyer, Kain and Wohl (1965), for instance, have argued that the provision of separate lanes for buses, supplemented by central monitoring and control, might have a dramatic effect. Even a simple feature such as the 700 feet platforms of the BARTD rail system to permit faster loading can have a marked influence on urban transport efficiency.

Interdependence between transportation and spacial structure

One of the main reasons why urban economic analysis often appears so complex is that within cities, everything seems to depend on everything else. Causation is rarely unidirectional, and interrelatedness is pervasive. This interdependence problem is found in a particularly striking form in the links between urban transportation, land use and the spatial structure of cities. Although we often treat urban transport as a problem in isolation, it must never be forgotten that this is merely an analytical convenience to be adopted sparingly. The interrelationships between transportation and location are intimate and inseparable. It is important to emphasize this point.

Since 75–90 per cent of all person trips involve either leaving or going home and 30–40 per cent involve the workplace, it is scarcely an exaggeration to argue that the urban transport problem arises because of the separation of home from work. The journey to work in a modern city results from comparatively free choice of residence and workplace, a choice which has become less restrictive with the greater number and variety of both and with new means of transportation (especially, of course, the motor car). If employment opportunities are centralized and if workers behave alike and choose to live in homogeneous concentrated areas a public transport system can cope. But urban change, both in the sense of expansion in city size and in terms of shifts in location, has marked repercussions on the journey to work and on the tasks facing the transport system.

As the city increases in size there is a tendency for the average length of the trip to increase. For instance, it is well known that if we assume that all jobs, services, shops and so forth are in the centre, if residential density is uniform and the city expands equally in all directions, then person–trip length increases at a rate equal to the square root of population expansion, that is if population and area quadruple, trip length doubles. Effects of changes in residential density are also significant; again assuming centralized work-places, trip length from home increases with the square root of the increase in land area per dwelling (Healy, 1965). Since not all journeys are to the centre and there are signs that economic activity is decentralizing, the rate of trip length increase tends to be below this rate. But decentralization of homes and work-places does not result in a shorter journey to work because homes and jobs neither move out at the same rate nor within the same sector of the city.

The evidence on decentralization is clear-cut in the United States; it is less so in Europe. In the United States we may observe absolute decentralization of population (this is a long-established historical fact; see for example, Schnore, 1965) and relative decentralization of activities (particularly of general services, leaving specialized functions in the city centre). In Britain, these trends have lagged behind those in the United

States. In the 1950s, although population was being relatively decentralized, there were even signs that activities were still being built up in city centres. In the past decade, however, the pace of suburbanization has accelerated and there have been some signs of economic functions, such as shopping centres and offices, moving away from the city centre. In any event, CBD employment in most major British cities has declined substantially. Even so, decentralization not only in Britain but on the continent has not been as marked as in the United States. The main consequences of diffusion of homes and workplaces have been a tendency for trip lengths to increase and for a higher proportion of journeys to work to be made by private car. These tendencies are clearly functions of the spacing of homes and workplaces and of the available routes and carriers connecting the two sites. The relationship between residential densities, the socio-economic characteristics of households, the spatial distribution of activities and employment centres on the one hand and traffic generation and modal split on the other is obvious, even if the details of their interaction are not fully understood. For instance, the very high proportion of trips by car on the west coast of America (especially in Los Angeles) is associated with low living densities, high incomes, dispersed employment centres, and moderate land values facilitating large scale road construction. In Chicago, on the other hand, a very high density of workplaces in the CBD has led to a high level of transit services and expensive parking charges, and the result is that commuting by public transport is very heavy.

At an even more generalized level, it is not difficult to see an historical interrelationship between transportation and urban development. The transport improvements of the nineteenth century led to agglomeration in cities, while the evolution of the motor car and modern forms of communication have made the exodus to the suburbs possible in the twentieth. In Britain the building of the Underground between 1890 and 1910 contributed to the expansion of London especially north of the river and permitted much higher densities than would have been possible with other means of transport. In New York the subway of 1905 opened up the Bronx, while the radial street railways of the late nineteenth and early twentieth centuries helped to create working class areas in Chicago, Philadelphia and Boston. The development of motor transport was associated with the growth of outer suburbs in Los Angeles, Detroit, Seattle and other cities. The dependence was not one way, since in many cases suburbanization itself created a new transport demand. The interaction is clearly illustrated by Lowry's analysis of Pittsburgh. Gains in transport efficiency resulting from improved roads and car parking facilities were soon absorbed by further dispersal of homes and workplaces. Dispersal enabled households to live at lower densities, and further increased the supremacy of the car.

Recognition of this interdependence has had a great impact on analysis of the urban transport problem. Initially, traffic engineers examined their design problems from the point of view of physical capacities and technical efficiency. It was realized by the early 1950s that this approach was inadequate. The urban transport system depends not only on the channels of movement but on the location of the terminal points (such as residences and workplaces), and the urban transport problem involves town planning as well as transport technology. The first major advance, the thesis that traffic is a function of land use, stems from Mitchell and Rapkin (1954). The argument is that different types of land use generate different traffic flows, and this changes the emphasis from the analysis of flows to the analysis of location and land use giving rise to them. Traffic engineers were inevitably forced into a study of human behaviour and choice. It was believed that if residential densities and the location and pattern of activities could be predicted then it might be possible to forecast the future volume of traffic using trip generation techniques such as gravity models (Iklé, 1954) and their variants (for example, by adapting an intervening opportunities model to the analysis of journeys to work).

This approach was adopted in many US transportation

studies particularly those sponsored by the Bureau of Public Roads. Examples include the plans developed for Chicago, Detroit, Penn–Jersey and the Tri-State New York Metropolitan Transportation Study. But the assumptions behind the Mitchell–Rapkin thesis are still unsatisfactory. It takes current and predicted land use patterns as given, and assumes that transport flows are dependent upon land use and activity patterns. It was not until the following decade that it was appreciated that the true relationship was one of interdependence, and that transport also influences land use patterns (Wingo and Perloff, 1961). This interdependence is especially marked in dynamic analysis. The development of the city over time will depend upon the sequence in which changes in land use and transportation occur. As Owen (1966, p. 225) has argued: 'We will have to use transportation resources to achieve better communities and community planning techniques to achieve better transportation. The combination would launch a revolutionary attack on urban congestion that is long overdue.'

Pricing and subsidy policies

As Thompson (1965, p. 335) has so effectively put it, we may view 'the urban transportation problem in a managerial context as two problems interrelated in time: pricing for today and investing for tomorrow.' At this point we are concerned with the first of these.

The most intractable problem in the field of urban transport is the congestion of motor vehicles in central areas of cities. Congestion creates appalling private and social costs: higher operating costs, losses in valuable time, more road accidents, air pollution, discomfort and inconvenience to pedestrians and residents, and so forth. The choices facing society are: to tolerate these losses; to reduce them by expensive investment in new roads; or to restrict road use in central areas. Pursuit of the first two courses is likely to result in further inefficiency – although it should be recognized that some level of congestion on particular facilities may be desirable (Kain, 1969) – and only the third choice offers the probability of improvement in the allocation of resources. Although there are other methods of restricting motor traffic use (parking prohibitions or restricting roads or lanes to certain types of traffic), control by price is much the most effective and the easiest to justify on efficiency grounds.

There are three broad pricing strategies which could be employed. They are, in ascending order of importance: taxes on suburban and dispersed living; subsidies to public transport; and various methods of increasing the costs of motoring, including road pricing and car parking charges. The first of these can be dealt with very briefly. The idea is to make residents in suburban areas pay the full cost of low density living (refuse disposal, streets, sewage, etc.); many urban services are more costly to supply to outlying areas. The long-run effect of this may be to encourage high density centripetal living, without which public transport is uneconomic. The difficulty with this course of action (though it might be desirable on other grounds) is that it is a very indirect way of tackling the urban transport problem, it may be ineffective and, even if it were not, would only take effect in the very long run.

Much more feasible is the possibility of subsidizing public transport. The general case for this rests on the view that it is much cheaper to provide facilities for public transport than for private cars, yet without subsidies or full cost charges on private cars it will usually be cheaper for the commuter to go by car. The most specific justification is that mass transit facilities may be subject to increasing returns to scale, and that only through subsidies will it be possible for the public to gain the benefits. Several types of subsidy are possible. Some suggest that capital costs should be subsidized, leaving operating costs to be covered by fares. Others suggest that a subsidy in terms of per passenger-mile or seat-mile would be more appropriate. There is even a case for free public transport: it would relieve traffic congestion and even benefit the commuter who still prefers his car; it would increase the number of passengers and therefore reduce the cost per passenger-mile;

it would reduce operating costs by savings on collection costs. In selecting an appropriate subsidy, we should bear in mind the uncertainty of mass transit investment decisions, the extremely long time horizon, and the effects of technical change and of shifts in population and industry. Subsidies should accordingly favour those projects which maximize the use of existing capital, which are reversible so that failures can be abandoned at very little cost, and which foreshadow or take account of future trends in transport technology. Whatever subsidy is adopted, it is doubtful whether such measures can in themselves solve the urban transport problem. Consumer preferences for private transport may be so strong that even free public transport may divert only a relatively small proportion of commuters from the car.

If this conclusion is correct, the best hope of restraining congestion is through some method of taxing the motorist. There are several feasible alternatives here. There are many arguments in favour of such an approach, not all of which are closely tied to the urban transport question. These arguments are usually stronger when they relate to direct road pricing rather than to cruder methods of pricing. Road pricing will not only help to decongest roads in the city centre, it could also in time encourage the dispersal of central locations. It is flexible, offering a means of virtually separating buses from cars on very congested streets and it gives some scope for dealing with the peak problem. Most important of all, road pricing and its variants can improve the allocation of resources. It may reduce the externalities arising from urban land use. It may provide a more reliable guide to transport investment decisions than cost-benefit analysis and other techniques, and, on a wider scale, it may reduce the arbitrary element in town planning decisions which result from the absence of or imperfections in urban markets for housing, land, roads, etc.

In spite of the advantages, there are difficulties in a policy of using price to improve the efficiency of urban transport. If some kind of marginal cost pricing is adopted, for example, we need to worry about the theory of second best. It has long been accepted that introducing an element of marginal cost pricing into one part of a set of monopolistic or imperfectly competitive markets will not necessarily lead to an improvement in welfare and a move towards optimality. However, it is probable that the adverse effects attributable to second-best influences are much less critical in urban transport than in other spheres. The other difficulties are more practical. The time and locational peaks in traffic flows complicate the design of a rational price structure. Measurement of income and price elasticities and the cross-elasticities of demand is so difficult that price elasticity is often ignored. There is also the possibility, suggested by Harris (1965), that the elasticity of demand may be insufficient for pricing to have much of an impact on road use. Finally, reduction of road congestion may result in such an improvement in service (that is traffic flow) that demand is soon restored to its previous levels.

There are several methods of restricting urban road use by raising the costs of motoring. These include tolls, fuel taxation, differential licence fees, car parking charges and direct road pricing.[3] Of these, the latter two are the most important. The other methods have serious drawbacks, apart from their crudity. Tolls are not very practicable in highly urbanized areas since queues may lead to congestion and collection costs will be heavy. Fuel taxation does have the advantage that it makes a charge proportional to road use in vehicular miles, but this is more than offset by its failure to take account of congestion or of variations in road construction costs. Differential licence fees by type of area is a crude device which also presents severe practical difficulties in regard to place of registration relative to places of use.

Car parking charges are a reasonably satisfactory short-term solution to the urban traffic congestion problem, though it is difficult to manipulate them to reflect the social costs of congestion due to motor vehicles. We may draw a distinction

3. It is, of course, feasible to deploy a mix of different methods. Walters (1961) suggested the use of fuel taxes, urban mileage taxes and special tolls.

between the administrative approach based on differential treatment for different types of vehicles and for short- and long-term parking, and an economic approach according to which allocation is decided solely by price. On the whole, the latter approach is preferable. It avoids having to distinguish between 'essential' and 'non-essential' traffic. If prices are set above costs the long-period parker will be deterred. Additional possibilities are: extension of parking controls beyond central areas and reducing spaces provided in streets below the limit set by the traffic flow; controlling the amount of parking space provided by companies and institutions located in central areas; adjusting times and charges so as to equate demand with capacity and to create enough spare space to reduce the need for cruising.

A generally preferred solution is to adopt some method of direct road pricing which will in effect be a congestion tax. The case for such a tax is that commuters pay only the private costs of motoring not the social costs, and also that some road users would value the benefits gained at less than the social marginal costs imposed on other road users. Road pricing aims at making motorists pay for congestion costs. These are usually strictly defined as the costs imposed by road users on other road users. This is only one component of social costs, since the social costs of heavy traffic flows, falling on pedestrians and nearby residents, are excluded. Thus, it is misleading to say that a congestion tax of this kind is equivalent to marginal social cost pricing.

How can we measure congestion?[4] Congestion costs include the value of lost time and increased operating costs due to delays and traffic jams (fuel, brakes, tyres, engine wear, etc.). The usual approach is to assume that unit costs are inversely related (sometimes proportionately) to speed. Charlesworth and Paisley (1959) suggested a method for estimating the costs

4. Buchanan (1963) in effect assumed either that congestion could not be measured or that road pricing was not the way to deal with it. This is implicit in his arbitrary distinction between 'optional' and 'essential' traffic, and in his concept of 'intolerable' congestion.

(excluding taxes) of declining speeds falling on the individual operator, while Smeed (1961) derived a formula that estimated, on the assumption that the relation between speed and traffic flow was linear, the 'public costs' imposed by given low speeds. Similar formulae have been used by Roth (1966), Hewitt (1964), Johnson (1964) and others. Most calculations of this kind include a term for the valuation of travel time, and this opens up a thorny and unsettled question. It is usually necessary to assign a relatively high value to travel time by car since, unlike with public transport, it is difficult to use this time for leisure or for work. One suggestion is to estimate the tolls that drivers would be prepared to pay to save time, though a drawback here is that drivers may prefer the newer toll roads.

If we assume for simplification that congestion costs are the only social cost imposed, then it may be argued that making the motorist pay for congestion will attempt to equate marginal private and social costs. Walters (1961) suggested that an efficient solution would equate private and social costs if it simultaneously satisfied the demand curve, so that

$$P = MC_s = MC_p (1 + \varepsilon_{MC_p}),$$

when P equals the price, MC_s is the marginal social cost, MC_p is the marginal private cost and ε_{MC_p} equals the elasticity of the marginal private cost curve. That marginal social costs will always exceed marginal private costs in urban congested conditions follows from the fact that the curve relating average traffic delay to traffic flow will be rising. Thus, the average delay suffered by a car will be less than the additional delay it imposes on all traffic.

Should congestion cost pricing be implemented, and if so, how should it be done? One suggestion is to have a *lower* general level of motor taxation (corresponding to real costs under uncongested conditions), supplemented by charging for road use under congested conditions. This might not restrict traffic sufficiently. Some have argued that for efficient allocation marginal cost pricing is normally a *minimum* level for appropriate charges. The reasoning behind this is that a desirable traffic flow is usually less than the capacity flow. This leads on to the argument made in some quarters that road pricing should be based on demand rather than on cost considerations. The case for this is two-fold. Firstly, there are the difficulties of assigning private and social costs and the technical problems involved in collection of charges. Secondly, and the more relevant in this context, if we set out the community's transportation planning goals it should then be possible to fix a price for road use which chokes off demand enough to ensure that these goals are achieved. Although it may be assumed that such a price will normally exceed marginal cost, the implementation problem remains difficult since estimating the price elasticity of demand for urban motor transport may not be much easier than assigning costs to users of urban transport facilities. Some writers object to congestion taxes on the ground that they might have unpredictable adverse consequences, to offset any benefits derived from improved road use (Sharp, 1966). For example, a tax on commercial vehicles might aggravate inflation rather than reduce congestion; lower paid workers might be forced to adopt slower journey to work modes; the tax may result in income transfers from town to country dwellers, and so on.

Another objection to road pricing used to be the technical problem of how to collect the charges. Tolls are cumbersome, while self-reporting is unreliable. This argument is no longer valid. Technical change has now made possible several means of charging for road use. Basically, there are two categories of device which may be employed. Each vehicle might be equipped with an identification unit which can be scanned by roadside equipment stationed at zone boundaries, records can be made and bills itemized (for further details see Vickrey, 1965). Alternatively, each car could be fitted with a meter, which displays an external signal to indicate functioning. The meter rate could be adjustable according to variations in traffic conditions, and could also function as a parking meter. The second method is the cheaper; the Smeed Panel on Road Pricing (Ministry of Transport, 1964) estimated a cost of less than £10 per vehicle, though additional costs might be involved in roadside activators and/or automated enforcement techniques. But the costs of such a scheme have to be placed in the context of the benefits. The Smeed Panel estimated a saving of resources as a result of direct road pricing in the region of £100–150 million, and this sum has probably increased substantially in the years since 1964.

Evaluation of transportation planning and investment

If pricing policy is the economic tactics of combatting the urban transport problem, investment is the economic strategy. This is not the place to examine the complex issues posed by transportation planning, but it is appropriate to mention some of the difficulties and to suggest how economic analysis has a role in clarifying some of the problems. Since urban motorways and mass public transit facilities may cost £5–12 million per mile, and the cost of implementing the Buchanan programme for building environmental areas in British towns and cities was estimated at over £20,000 million, the scale of urban transport investments clearly makes it impossible to ignore this problem altogether.

Transportation planning is fraught with dangers. For instance, there is a temptation to opt for the extremes of pure strategies – such as all-out accommodation of the car on the one hand or banning the car from the CBD on the other. The first of these is impossible. It would absorb too much space for road-building, require too much destruction of the fabric of our cities and displace too many families from their homes. The second alternative is not very practicable, and is probably too extreme. In almost all circumstances, a mix of different modes of travel and strategies is called for. A related point is the need to avoid the premature dismissal of feasible alternatives. Such alternatives might include a new mass transit facility, direct road pricing, peak hour tolls for motorists, and so on. It is often too easy to rule possibilities of this kind out of court on some pretext such as their being politically unacceptable, or too costly. All this suggests that a systems analysis approach, involving an assessment of the costs and effectiveness of a wide range of alternatives, is more desirable in this field than cost-benefit and other narrowly circumscribed techniques.

There are other difficulties. What criteria should be used in the evaluation of transport investments? Beesley and Walters (1970) argue for measurable criteria such as travel time, outlays on road services and cost of accidents avoided, while other writers, such as Kain (1969), warn against the use of low-level criteria, such as time and fuel savings, and instead press for the wider if more nebulous criterion of maximization of vehicle-user benefits which might approximate to maximum net benefits for the community. The goals of transportation planning may be multiple and complex, not easily reduced to a single quantifiable objective. Another danger is a preoccupation with long-range problems, such as the transport system of twenty or thirty years hence, neglecting both what can be done with existing facilities and the path of adjustment towards the future state. As Kain argues:

For several reasons, not the least of which is the discount rate, the greatest potential benefits are those that might be obtained from current decisions about the use of existing facilities or those to be built in the near future. . . . It follows that the most detailed and sophisticated analyses and planning should be concerned with improving the use of existing urban transport capacity and near term investment decisions.

Moreover, to the extent that long-run considerations are critical it is apparent that transport planning cannot be undertaken in isolation. In the urban economy the transport system and the land use and urban structure configuration are simultaneously determined, and the interaction between them must be taken explicitly into account. As a result, long-range transportation planning must not be divorced from urban planning in general.

Although cost-benefit techniques are widely employed in transport investment decision-making, their application in this field raises problems. For example, it is insufficient to estimate whether a particular investment would yield an excess of discounted benefits over discounted costs or to rank projects according to such criteria. Since pricing and subsidies are often an inevitable component of a planned transport system, it is often necessary to *assign* benefits and costs as well as to estimate their total. The number of alternatives that can be assessed with cost-benefit analysis at any one time is very limited. Budget constraints and ranking over time also present problems, though these are not insuperable. The first difficulty can be met by fitting the programme size to the constrained budget by varying the discount rate; if there is a wide disparity between the appropriate discount rate and the rate of return in the private sector, this is a sign that something is amiss with the budget constraint. The second problem can be solved by exploring the implications of bringing forward or delaying individual projects, for the correct criterion is the maximization of the difference between discounted benefits and costs for the programme over the planning period as a whole.

Another problem that frequently occurs in transportation planning is what distinction should be made between capital costs and operating costs in an urban transport investment decision. To take much notice of this distinction can be highly dangerous. For instance, operating costs are often unconstrained on the ground that future costs can be met from future revenues. This would give a bias in favour of projects which had a lower capital intensity, regardless of whether they yielded substantial community benefits or not. Distortions can also arise when massive central government aid is brought in to support the financing of urban transport investments.

It would be wrong to infer from these qualifications that transport planning is a hopeless task or that economics has no relevance to it. It is true that community objectives relating to the urban transport system may be very wide, and that some of them cannot be translated into monetary values or easily incorporated in a cost-benefit analysis. Moreover, these goals may have to be determined by collective value judgements. Nevertheless, economic analysis will continue to have a substantial role. This role can take many forms, of which the following are merely examples: how to minimize the costs of achieving stated objectives; assessing the changes in measurable benefits obtained by adjusting the level of costs; studying the time path of achieving specified goals and the optimal spatial phasing of components of a transport system; estimating the effects of programmes with different capital intensities; designing performance standards and checking on operational efficiency; and possibly most important of all, examining the trade-offs between different objectives, benefits and costs (safety versus speed, air pollution versus cost, travel time versus road costs, and so on).

5 Urban Renewal

General comments

The term 'urban renewal' was coined by the American housing economist Miles Colean about 1950. It has several possible meanings. Weimer and Hoyt (1966) suggest that UR covers three types of programme: *rehabilitation*, that is bringing substandard structures up to a prescribed standard; *conservation*, involving both rehabilitation and spot clearance in order to upgrade an area; and *redevelopment* – the demolition, clearance and reconstruction of an entire area. Grebler (1965, p. 13) defines UR as 'a deliberate effort to change the urban environment through planned, large-scale adjustment of existing city areas to present and future requirements for urban living and working'. More precise is the Medhurst and Parry Lewis (1969) statement that UR means 'extensive demolition of property, most of it old, in a way that clears a large area of ground and so permits the planning and construction of a new set of buildings, streets and space'. More often than not, such renewal takes place in or near a town centre.

A crucial feature of UR is the involvement of government. Why public action and public subsidies are necessary to renovate deteriorating areas calls for a brief discussion of what might be called the economic theory of slums. One aspect of this is aggregate analysis of cumulative income decline in core areas, and this is discussed below. Another aspect is what happens at the microeconomic level, that is the individual structure and the behaviour of the individual property owner. The main lines of the argument have been advanced by many, but particularly by Davis and Whinston (1961). Most buildings can be maintained in a good state of repair provided that their owners are willing to undertake the maintenance expenditures required. Consequently, structures decline in quality because owners permit them to do so. How does this create slums? The reason is to be found in the existence of externalities, or neighbourhood effects, arising from the spatial proximity of buildings. One of the determinants of the market value of a particular property is the quality of the neighbourhood in which it is located, that is a spillover effect. This means that an owner obtains the highest return from his property if it is undermaintained while others in the area are well maintained, and conversely, he receives a lower return if he upkeeps a property in a deteriorating area. In the latter case it pays him to maintain his property in good condition only if adjacent properties are also upgraded, and in an atomistic market this condition will not be fulfilled. For instance, consider an area in which some houses are allowed to deteriorate. If this is not checked, the spillover effects will reduce the market value of adjacent houses. This will discourage further investment and eventually essential repairs, and deterioration will spread. This process leads ultimately to a low-level equilibrium, the slum.

There are also other factors which can lead to deterioration, especially proximity to non-residential activities. Certain types of non-residential uses lower the quality of nearby residential sites. More important is the reluctance of property owners near non-residential activities to spend much on maintenance if they expect their property to be ultimately absorbed as non-residential uses expand. There may be intermediate steps on the way to complete deterioration. An obvious instance is for property owners and landlords to make density-increasing conversions which raise the rental value of an individual property but also accelerate the rate of deterioration.

In most cases, private owners have no incentive to redevelop an area themselves. This is sometimes because higher returns are obtainable from investment elsewhere, but on the above analysis the main reason is the interdependence of investment decisions. UR can work only if the public sector assumes the cost of private spillovers and substitutes a public–private investment mix for the operations of the market. Whether UR should then be undertaken depends upon whether the sum of its benefits exceeds the sum of its costs. This leads on to the complex and unsettled question of the relevance of cost-benefit analysis to UR.

The general difficulties arising from the application of cost-benefit techniques are well known (Prest and Turvey, 1965). These are multiplied in a UR context. The 'intangibles' are particularly difficult to measure. How great are the social costs generated by slum living, and how can these be weighed against the attachment of families to their neighbourhood area? Abrams (1965) goes so far as to argue that 'Financial benefits cannot be offset against social costs nor an increase in revenues juxtaposed against the myriad peoples evicted from their homes.' Moreover, the time horizon in UR projects is so long, sometimes more than twenty years, that the balance of costs and benefits at the end of the project could differ dramatically from those estimated when the investment decision is made. Another factor is that a UR project often serves multiple goals, and these goals may be ranked in such a way that the weights attached to each would result in a very different evaluation of benefits from one obtained via an aggregate measure of monetary benefits. Such goals include: profitability on private or social account; maximizing short-run benefits to city tax revenues; the demonstration effect of setting new urban standards in design; long-run income gain for the city population. A related point is that political and community pressures cannot be ignored. Decisions relating to UR are in the main taken by local governments, and if the political costs of a particular UR decision are great they are very likely to outweigh even a substantial excess of economic benefits over economic costs.

Finally, a serious consideration with UR is that redistributive effects are so important, and figure so prominently in UR goals, that the incidence of benefits and costs may be more critical than their aggregate value. Central government subsidies mean that in most cases increased tax revenues from new structures for the city government will exceed its share of project costs. But this does not necessarily mean an overall social gain. We must take into account the tax losses during the course of the project, the possibility that the new buildings might have been put up elsewhere, and the likelihood that a city government, formulating its own project from the narrow viewpoint of its finances and residents, may make suboptimal public investment decisions. It is difficult to disentangle the transfer payment effects from any potential real income gain. Moreover, a UR programme is often justified as a device for helping the poor, yet evidence from several countries, particularly the United States, suggests that poor families and small businesses are often the chief victims. These considerations suggest that a preferred criterion would be maximization of welfare among a relevant population (where the relevant population is that of the whole urbanized region not of the central city or the small neighbourhood where the actual project is located) rather than maximization of property values in the relevant area. But even if on pragmatic grounds we choose to ignore the quagmire of the impossibility of interpersonal comparisons, such a criterion still raises enormous problems since it would require classification of affected persons into homogeneous groups and an attempt to evaluate the cost/benefit implications for each group.

Despite the obstacles, there have been a few attempts to cast these problems in cost-benefit terms, notably by Rothenberg (1967). He recognizes the difference in precision between the estimates of budget costs and those of other costs and benefits, and as a result defines 'benefits' as all consequences of UR both negative (undesirable) and positive, and restricts costs to the financing of the project. We may write the following identities:

$$C_{GP} = C_A + C_R$$
$$C_A = V_o + I_o$$
$$TC = I_o + C_R.,$$

Thus $TC = (C_A - V_o) + C_R = C_{GP} - V_o.$

Also $TB = (V_1 - V_o) + E + \Delta C_S,$

where

C_{GP} = gross project cost

C_A = acquisition cost of property on the site

C_R = expenditure of resources other than acquisition cost

V_0 = market value of land acquired on the site

V_1 = market value of land after renewal

I_0 = market value of buildings acquired with the site

TC = total resource costs of project

TB = total benefits (both positive and negative)

E = spillover effects (normally positive such as the increased value of neighbouring property)

ΔC_S = fall in the social costs of slums (which may be positive or negative)

I_0 is lost to society as a result of the project but not V_0. Rothenberg accepts that E and ΔC_S are very difficult to measure but suggests that the gap between TC and $(V_1 - V_0)$ may help the decision-making process. Rough empirical tests suggested that there were marked economies of scale in UR projects since the deficiency of measured benefits relative to resource costs declined steadily with increasing C_{GP}.

That there might be substantial economies of scale in UR is easily understood. The redevelopment of large tracts of land can raise productivity by opening up additional options for development; for example, an efficient office building may need to be of a substantial minimum site size, or a large residential development project may offer certain scale economies such as a centralized heating plant or enough demand to justify the building of shops and other service establishments. Also, large scale redevelopment can 'internalize the externalities' by reducing spillover costs from dilapidated property by swallowing it up in the project while raising the value of property on the fringe of the redevelopment. Of course, these are *economies* of scale. There may in some cases be adverse scale effects, such as destroying the essential character of part of a city, but such effects are impossible to measure. Moreover, it depends on the quality and the design of the new buildings and layout. The physical shape of a city is always changing, and some, if not all, changes are for the better.

Whereas there is hope of being able to measure changes in property values after redevelopment and spillover effects, the inability to assign a monetary measure to the social costs of slums and to the benefits derived from removing them means that cost-benefit analysis can be no more than a rough-and-ready guide to UR decisions. So many of the variables to be considered refer to things which cannot appear in any market, such as social values and neighbourhood ties. Moreover, it is not very meaningful to compare *per capita* service costs before and after UR nor to use the ratio of government expenditures to revenues in slum areas as an indicator of government 'losses'. In the first case it may be simply that the location where the costs are incurred has changed, while the second may reflect progressive distribution effects much more than real social costs. On the other hand, even if redevelopment induces slums elsewhere, any *net* fall in slum occupancy should tend to reduce social costs. But there are other difficulties. It is difficult to separate the costs of slums from those of other highly intercorrelated factors such as poverty. For instance, some analysts have tried to measure UR gains in terms of reductions of fire hazards, improvement in health indices, fall in crime rates, and so forth. But how can we be sure that fire risk, poor health and delinquency are the results of the slums *per se*?

Another problem in cost-benefit appraisals of UR is that the decision-makers are prone to make isolated judgements, neglecting the social opportunity cost of achieving alternative ends with their budgets. Since failure to consider alternative programmes will lead to misallocation of resources, it is clear that social net benefits rather than gross benefits are the correct criteria. Moreover, UR schemes are shrouded in uncertainty. In the United Kingdom, for instance, the renewal of town centres is the joint product of partnership between private developers (using their capital and knowledge of the market) and the planning authorities. Assuming conflict between commercial considerations and 'good planning', each UR scheme is determined by bargaining between developers aimed at maximizing returns and planners seeking the most desirable layout or the maximum amount of non-profitable assets, for example roads and open spaces. The solution here is not only indeterminate but is not finally settled until the scheme is under way and after the basic investment decisions have been made. Neither group is fully informed, and in particular there is the insoluble problem of accommodating current schemes to long-term plans yet to be devised. For these and all the other reasons discussed above, a cost-benefit approach to individual UR projects is unsatisfactory and fails to place the UR problem within the wider context of the general strategy of city planning. If we wish to base decisions primarily on economic efficiency criteria a more effective approach to the UR problem would be the use of systems analysis. This has several advantages over cost-benefit techniques: a rational consideration of a wide range of feasible alternatives; measurement of the least-cost method of achieving specified objectives *or* the maximization of returns from a given budget expenditure; circumvention of the need to employ a single measure of benefits.

The theory of blight

Urban blight is associated most of all with a decline in the income of central areas and with a tendency for this decline to become cumulative. This trend displays itself in the familiar blight phenomena: failure to maintain property, a widening gap between neighbourhood tax receipts and expenditures on services, out-migration of high income residents, and urban poverty. A neat and simple model to describe the process of cumulative income decline in blight areas has been developed by Baumol (1963). His model is based on first order difference equations.

Assuming that blight is measurable, and that B_t is an index of blight in period t, we may express the state of blight as a decreasing function of the level of *per capita* income, Y_t:

$$B_t = g Y_t, \qquad \frac{dg}{dY} < 0. \qquad (1)$$

Thus, for example, blight will accelerate the migration of wealthy families with adverse effects on central area incomes.

We can then choose from alternative hypotheses. The first is that blight affects the *level* of *per capita* income,

$$Y_{t+1} = G_1 B_t, \qquad \frac{dG_1}{dB} < 0. \qquad (2)$$

Substituting **1** into **2** we obtain

$$Y_{t+1} = G_1 g Y_t = F_1 Y_t, \frac{dF_1}{dY} > 0. \qquad (3)$$

The second hypothesis is that blight increases the rate of decline in income, so that

$$Y_{t+1} - Y_t = G_2 B_t, \qquad \frac{dG_2}{dB} < 0. \qquad (4)$$

Substituting **1** into **4**

$$Y_{t+1} - Y_t = G_2 g Y_t = f Y_t, \qquad \frac{df}{dY} > 0, \qquad (5)$$

or

$$Y_{t+1} = f Y_t - Y_t = F_2 Y_t,$$

where F_2 equals $(f - 1)$. Generalizing **3** and **5**

$$Y_{t+1} = F Y_t \qquad (6)$$

This is a standard first order non-linear difference equation.

We can identify a stable case and an unstable case. In Fig. 2 these are represented by the curves $F_s Y_t$ and $F_u Y_t$ respectively. In the unstable case ($F_u Y_t$) if *per capita* income falls below the critical level Y_K, say to Y_J, cumulative deterioration becomes irreversible unless the urban government intervenes ($Y_1 < Y_J$). Economic conditions in the blighted core area get worse, *per capita* income falls (Y_1, Y_2, . . .), and income declines along the path ABC. . . . In the stable case (F_s, Y_t), below Y_0 *per capita* income declines but within firm limits; Y_t asymptotically approaches the lower limit Y_K but never falls below this level.

What determines whether a particular situation is stable or unstable? In terms of Fig. 2 the answer depends on whether at its point of intersection with the 45° line, the slope of the F function is greater or less than 45°. A slope greater than one means instability, while a slope of less than one implies stability. The model in which blight affects the *level* of income (equation 3) is necessarily unstable because dF_1/dY_t is positive. In equation 5, however, $dF_2/dY_t = df/dY_t - 1$, and this has an ambiguous sign. A stable case may result in certain circumstances. For example, if a fall in income leads to only a slight increase in blight which in turn has only minor effects on the rate of income decline, then dg/dY and dG_2/dB are both small and hence df/dY (that is $dG_2/dB \times dg/dY$) is also small.

The stable cumulative process occurs quite often in practice.

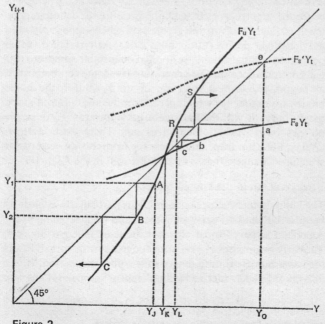

Figure 2

Thus, in Fig. 2 we might hypothesize an initially satisfactory situation with the function $F_s' Y_t$ yielding a stable equilibrium level at e. Let this equilibrium be disturbed by an exogenous downward shift in the F-curve from $F_s' Y_t$ to $F_s Y_t$. This might be caused by autonomous changes in residential area preferences, such as an increased desire to live in the suburbs.[1] As a result of the shift, income declines cumulatively from Y_o towards Y_K.

The lower income limit of the stable model compared with the theoretical zero level of the unstable model might suggest that the former is much the lesser of two evils. Except where a high equilibrium income level is maintained, this is by no means true. First, the lower income limit of the F_s function may be very low. Second, income will not be allowed to fall to zero in unstable situations, since urban renewal agencies will be forced to intervene. Indeed, the pressure for action may be much stronger than in the stable case where apparently mild but insidious deterioration may delay action. Third, when policies to combat blight are applied in unstable situations, expansion may become self-generating if income can be pushed up beyond the critical level Y_K, say to Y_L. But in the stable model, no matter how high *per capita* income is raised along the F_S curve it will decline again back towards Y_K once the policies have worked themselves out. There exists a 'low-level equilibrium trap', and to escape from this we need major structural changes, that is an upward shift in the F_S curve.

Urban renewal in the United States

The United States' experience of UR is particularly interesting because UR had an early start there and because some of the American schemes most clearly exhibit its inherent dangers. The early beginnings (1949) were due to many factors. UR was seen as a pump-priming device in the post war period. It was also considered attractive by municipal governments (as a way

1. Incidentally, this model can be used to analyse the fiscal problems of an urban public transport system where, say, the attainment of a critical level of car ownership can shift the F curve.

of protecting and improving the declining tax base of the central city) and by businessmen and property owners who were concerned about the prospects of stagnating sales and property values. It has also been argued that the wealthy and intellectual elites in urbanized America gave strong support to UR because of their strong economic and social attachment to city centres. A rather different element in the situation is that suburbanization began earlier and went further in the United States than elsewhere and this probably accelerated the deterioration of core residential areas. It is not surprising therefore that the main emphasis has been on renewal of residential areas, though often to redevelop with commercial properties. All these points emphasize the argument that UR is a weapon of the central city in its fight against the suburbs.

That the United States should have led the way with UR, which involves potential conflict between individual rights and governmental powers, is at first sight paradoxical in one of the most capitalistic of economies. For instance, the powers of eminent domain (that is compulsory purchase) are developed further there than in most other countries, particularly since 1954 when these powers were extended to permit land to be acquired for private use as well as public use. These powers have been exercised in a way which has allowed large tracts to be acquired; this has led to the criticism that operations on this scale (the 'bulldozer approach') have destroyed the character of small neighbourhoods (Jacobs, 1961). The conflict between the State and the individual is serious because it relates not only to private property rights but also to the disturbance of families and businesses, and this dislocation has been more painful in the United States than elsewhere. For example, the obligations to relocate displaced families have not been enforced and, despite official statements to the contrary, many families (particularly in minority groups) have had to accept sub-standard housing. Moreover, only one-half of families received compensation, usually very meagre sums (Anderson (1964) quotes an average of seventy-one dollars per family); business firms have not fared much better. This suggests a tendency to pull back from the brink of full scale intervention, a view supported by the fact that public ownership of land is not permitted in the UR programme. Once a project ends, the land and buildings on it are sold to private developers at 30 per cent of the acquisition and improvement costs, and two-thirds of the city's loss is made up by a direct cash subsidy from the federal government. Thus, we find in the United States' UR programme both paradox and compromise: great powers and funds to acquire and clear areas, but few resources to deal with the problems of people affected; heavy public subsidies yet eventual sale to private enterprise.

By the end of 1965, some 1700 projects had been approved in 800 cities. Yet the projects took a long time to complete (an average of twelve years), and only a small proportion had been completed. Perhaps three-quarters of a million people had been evicted and moved, and more than 50,000 businesses had been forced to relocate or go out of business. Yet UR accounted for only 0·2 per cent of total construction, and total federal grants authorized amounted to little more than eight billion dollars. Since 1965, however, the pace of renewal has accelerated.

There have been many accusations levied against the federal programme. Some of the most important include: it has been regressive in its effects by reducing the volume of low-income housing while increasing high-rent, tall apartments, and by forcing the poor to move into worse and more costly accommodation; slums have been merely shifted about rather than removed; it has destroyed some of the social and physical fabric and the life and character of cities, and often put in its place unimaginative concentrations of a single function (all housing in one area, all shops in another, for example); public subsidies have been used to create a situation in which private developers may make huge capital gains; much of the new construction in the UR programme would have been put up elsewhere in the city. It would take too long to examine these charges in detail. There is no doubt that a sound UR programme could benefit from the mistakes made in the United

States by adopting the following schemes: more emphasis should be placed on the provision of housing for low-income groups and less on provision of expensive housing and commercial development; relocation for families and firms should be made easier and less expensive; physical renewal should be integrated with social planning and the war against poverty; there should be a change in a system in which most of the costs fall on the public exchequer while most of the benefits are reaped by private developers.

Urban renewal in Great Britain

This is not an appropriate place to survey the historical development of UR in Great Britain; it is too complicated a story. But it is necessary to make a few general observations and to draw one or two contrasts with experience in the United States.

The legislative foundations of UR in Great Britain are scattered over several acts. There is a long series of housing legislation through the interwar period and since 1945, and quite substantial slum clearance programmes were mounted even in the 1930s. A more explicit UR policy was established under a sequence of Town and Country Planning Acts stemming from the Act of 1944; local governments were called upon to prepare not only overall development plans but also comprehensive redevelopment schemes. The basis of the policy is the compulsory purchase powers of the local authorities and a direct system of national long-term loans and grants to these authorities, mainly by way of annual subsidies. These subsidies lean heavily towards residential renewal, and this is the main reason for a division of interest in UR in the United Kingdom: most housing renewal schemes derive from local authority initiative, while many central non-residential schemes are initiated by private developers. Despite the array of legislation, there is no coordinated national UR policy, and renewal is initiated at the local level, though with central cooperation and assistance in regard to housing, road-building and planning. An important difference compared with the United

States is that cities in Britain have very often retained the ownership of urban land and leased sites for private use.

Although 1·153 million houses were demolished in Great Britain in the period from 1955 to 1970, the pace of urban renewal has nevertheless been quite slow. There are many reasons for this. Funds have been short, partly because of the limited taxing powers of local authorities, partly because UR has had only a small share of general national grants owing to other demands on resources for building roads and other developments, and partly because acquisition costs of sites have been rising faster than grants. The critical housing shortage over most of the postwar period has made it difficult to pursue a rapid policy of area-wide redevelopment. Relocation procedures are more firmly established than in the United States, for instance the need to rehouse displaced slum tenants, and this has limited the scope and speed of UR in Britain. Planning delays in the approval of schemes and cumbersome machinery have allowed private property companies to have the pick of UR areas. Local authorities have often been slow in preparing schemes, and have tended to award projects to the highest bidder with little regard for planning quality considerations. Finally, the few cities which have followed through large ambitious central redevelopment schemes, Birmingham for instance, have tended to adopt very long-term projects and have been too inflexible in making modifications in response to changing conditions and requirements.

Alternatives

A UR programme should not be regarded as the unique prescription for potentially blighted areas. There are alternative measures available particularly for residential blight. Of these, rehabilitation of deteriorating dwellings is the most obvious. In Britain, for instance, there has been a considerable shift of emphasis towards rehabilitation with the new improvement grants under the Housing Act of 1969. About one-quarter of the housing stock in Britain lacks at least one of the basic amenities, and the increased improvement grants reflect the feeling that families should not have to wait for long periods in uninhabitable dwellings until they can be provided with new homes. However, improvement is not a perfect substitute for renewal. The conditions under which improvement grants are offered are strictly defined, and there is little help given to promoting repairs and maintenance for houses which fall outside the approved categories. Yet subsidies in this sphere, for example by giving tax allowances, could be much cheaper than wholesale redevelopment at a later date. The feasibility of preserving areas by widespread rehabilitation and a little spot clearance for the worst substandard structures depends, of course, on the state of dilapidation of the area's housing stock. Action of this kind needs to be taken early. Moreover, to be successful, improvement schemes have to be enforced on area-wide scale. Leeds, for example, designated sixty-six improvement areas between 1955 and 1966 in which all houses (except in cases of hardship) had to be brought up to standard, either by improvement grants or local authority acquisition. The 1969 Housing Act made provision for grants for environmental improvement, and by the end of 1970, 102 general improvement areas (covering 35,700 dwellings) had been declared in England and Wales. A policy of rehabilitation may be worth pursuing even if it prolongs the life of an area only for a moderate period. In most cases improvements do not postpone the need for replacement indefinitely. For these reasons comprehensive urban renewal and a rehabilitation programme tend to be complementary rather than alternatives.

Another line of attack is to lubricate the housing market so that the required physical changes will be brought about by decisions in the housing market rather than by compulsory purchase, eviction and clearance. Action can be taken on the demand side (rent subsidies or direct income payments to low income families) or on the supply side (expanding the public house-building sector or subsidizing credit to private builders) or by reducing market imperfections (rate or property tax reform, by-law and code enforcement, measures to end discrimination in housing). Of course, all these schemes are limited in scope in that they are applicable only to residential blight. Given deteriorating conditions in the commercial and business core of a city, there are few alternatives to wholesale redevelopment. Perhaps this does not matter very much since private developers are more willing to seize the opportunities for profitable commercial redevelopments than to enter the more risky field of residential renewal. In cases, however, where the local government takes a major interest in central redevelopment it has been argued that subsidies to the central city through UR programmes are an inefficient approach to the central city problem. The alternative which has been most canvassed, particularly in the United States in the Heller–Pechman revenue sharing plan (see Perloff and Nathan, 1968) is that the central government should give unconditional grants to cities on the basis of need and allow the cities to spend these grants as they think fit. Another possibility is that local government boundaries should not be regarded as permanent but should be redrawn so that the wealthy in the suburbs pay taxes to the city; this strengthens the case for large metropolitan regions. These issues relate more to urban fiscal problems than to UR (see ch. 6).

Some conclusions

Discussion of UR in Britain have been largely confined to two narrow problems: firstly, abstract technical arguments about the relative economic cost of rebuilding houses or modernization (Needleman, 1965, 1967 and 1969, Sigsworth and Wilkinson, 1967); secondly, emphasis on the social disturbances associated with urban renewal.

UR is not merely a question of delimiting blighted areas, and deciding whether they should be renovated or cleared and its population rehoused. The most satisfactory way to combat the UR problem is as part of a city-wide planning strategy, and particularly to meet incipient problem areas before they emerge. This requires more detailed investigation into the causes of urban blight (for example low incomes, age of structures, high costs of housing and of investment in blighted areas, class segregation of residential areas, reluctance of individual property owners to renovate unilaterally, environmental deficiencies) and into the measures necessary to prevent it. Perhaps even more important, it requires planners to have indicators sensitive to the dynamics of urban change at hand which enable them to identify potential blighted areas. Such indicators include the number of conversions and alterations, and also new housing units, granted planning permission by zone; vacancy surveys; and, possibly most valuable of all, zonal house price indices.

The problem is not solely one of physical renewal. Dilapidation of residential property may be a symptom rather than a cause of blight. If the links between urban blight and low incomes are recognized, then physical renewal programmes will need support from social renewal measures. These links raise certain questions. What are the implications of urban economic growth for income distribution in cities? Can we predict an area's capacity to develop slums from its level and distribution of income?

A more critical and detached view is needed of the thesis that relocation of slum inhabitants involves costly social disturbance. The usual argument is that relocation breaks down neighbourhood and community ties, and merely leads to social problems being removed from central slums to suburban estates. Conversely, renovation is often justified on the grounds that it induces stabilization of an area, it eases pressure on housing supply and is less likely to create a massive housing subsidy problem, it minimizes public expenditure, and it facilitates coordination between physical and social renewal. While there is some truth in these arguments, their force can be exaggerated. In particular, the breakdown of community ties can be overemphasized. For example, it may be argued that the nuclear family is a self-contained social unit, and that a proper environment in which it can develop (especially a comfortable home) is much more important than the retention of broader kinship and community ties. In other words, the breakdown in community ties has to be weighed against the convenience of a modern house, since even after renovation old properties are unlikely to compare in amenities with the new. Secondly, since renovation extends the life of an old house for only a limited period, the choice is usually between disturbance now or disturbance later. What are the grounds (other than economic) for putting off an inevitable decision? Furthermore, because a new house has a very long life (say a hundred years) the question becomes one of equity between generations. If, for example, the aged are particularly resistant to being rehoused, while young people and/or the next generation prefer the new environment of a suburb rather than old streets in central areas, the preferences of the old have to be balanced against those of the young. Sometimes the renovation of an old area is recommended on aesthetic grounds. When attractiveness or quaintness of outside appearance coincides with soundness and spaciousness of internal structures, this is all right. In many cases, however, the conservationist argument for houses is put by those who do not have to live in them. Finally, any harmful effects of relocation and breakdown of community ties can be alleviated by: rehousing, where appropriate, part of the displaced population on the cleared site; keeping communities together as far as possible during relocation; taking consumer preferences into account in providing new housing for displaced slum dwellers.

In many large cities UR expenditures may be lagging behind the development of new slums. If this is the case. it is very important to spend available budgets efficiently. Thus, we need more investigation into the criteria upon which UR priorities should be based. Also, the timing of action with regard to a particular area may be crucial. Firstly, in some cases if measures are taken soon enough renovation may be much cheaper and socially more effective than clearance and redevelopment. Secondly, even if it is decided that an area should be redeveloped, it does not follow that this is best done immediately. Other considerations have to be taken into account: whether or not there is slack in the construction industry, the level of compensation that will have to be paid now or in the future, the age distribution of the resident population (if the age distribution is skewed towards the old, fewer people may be *adversely* affected if we redevelop in ten years time rather than now).

It is sometimes argued that there are 'tipping points' in the development of urban areas. These may occur in two types of situation: when a 'mixed' area starts to go downhill (as in Baumol's unstable model of urban blight, 1967); when an old area attains a level of rehabilitation strong enough to ensure upgrading. 'Tipping points' of the second type may be of crucial importance because appropriate injections of public investment may encourage private investment in renovation – what Thompson (1965) calls the 'renewal accelerator'. The problem is complex since different types of public policy action (according to various site-plan layouts, for example) give rise to different degrees of risk and pay-off levels. Moreover, government action to stimulate private modernization may take varied forms, from renovation subsidies to investment in public services (the provision of new schools, for example).

Finally, it is wrong to overemphasize housing in UR. Urban blight is not confined to residential areas. Commercial blight may develop in areas with old, dilapidated industrial and commercial buildings, environmental deficiencies, over-strained and inadequate transport facilities, high site costs and rates, limited room for plant expansion. Moreover, there should be flexibility in land use allocation; there is no reason why cleared industrial land should not be used for housing, or why cleared slums should not make way for office buildings or other forms of commerce. Indeed, the provision of commercial buildings in core blighted areas would not necessarily use up much land and would be one possible way of attracting professional residents back to central areas. This attraction can be very important since UR problems often have a fiscal aspect, the need to increase the tax base. It is necessary to investigate what buildings or types of activity should be encouraged in the core blighted areas after demolition. Cost-benefit and opportunity cost criteria are unlikely to suggest new housing in every case.

6 The Fiscal Problems of Urban Governments

Local budget functions

The public sector has several distinct, if interrelated, objectives. These objectives can be related to three broad functions: the allocation branch to supplement the market mechanism in determining the allocation of economic resources; the distribution branch which is concerned with bringing about desired changes in the distribution of income and wealth; and the stabilization branch through which attempts are made to reconcile the goals of price stability, full employment and fast growth. The control of each branch must be undertaken on the assumption that the other two branches are being looked after independently and effectively.

Local governments should primarily be concerned with allocation; they are not equipped to deal with redistribution and stabilization. For instance, if local authorities were given redistributive functions their actions could be neutralized by out-migration of firms and households. Moreover, the central government's own income distribution objective would be frustrated if urban governments adopted explicit redistribution measures. Of course, it is virtually inevitable that local authority expenditure policies will have distributional side-effects, and the central government will have to do its best to predict these effects and to take them into account.

Similarly, urban government activities will have stabilization effects. These may be quite important with growing local authority capital budgets and depending on the timing of local government investment *vis-à-vis* fluctuations in general economic activity. Nevertheless, here too, responsibility should rest with the central government, though coordination between the central and local levels is desirable. What is clear is that urban governments are poor fiscal units for the pursuit of stabilization goals. There are many reasons for this: inflexibility in the short run of local needs for public goods and services; the risk of geographical leakages over local government boundaries that may create interarea equity problems; the lack of policy instruments and the existence of fiscal constraints. Most important of all, stabilization policies pursued by some local governments may have destabilizing effects on economic activity in others. For instance, locally initiated employment programmes may reduce interarea mobility of labour with harmful effects on locational efficiency.

The public sector has an allocative function because the market mechanism may fail to achieve an optimal allocation of resources. It may need to intervene to correct the effects of external economies and diseconomies of private actions, for instance in the pollution and traffic congestion fields. The public sector will certainly have to provide those goods and services which meet social wants. Social wants are met by services which are consumed by all, though the level of consumption may differ from one person to another. Since people cannot be excluded from the benefits of these services (street lighting and cleaning, for example), some individuals will not voluntarily pay for them. Thus, social wants cannot be satisfied by the market, and have to be supplied by the public sector, if at all.

Finally, governments may be concerned with merit wants. These are needs which can be met by the market, but where market forces may supply too much or too little from the point of view of society as a whole. The appropriate remedies are taxes and subsidies. In some cases the public sector may take direct responsibility for providing the services, in others private supply may be subsidized. An obvious illustration is where the government attempts to increase the allocation of resources to education, medical treatment and house-building, by public subsidies. Why do these matters concern urban governments? The simple reason is that in a multi-level fiscal

system, units of a particular size and organization will be more
fitted to provide certain types of service than others. Some
services can be most efficiently supplied by the central government, while others are best handled by regional and local
governments. The appropriate level in the fiscal hierarchy will
depend on several factors: the number and distribution of persons who benefit; the optimal administrative area for the service in question; scale economies and diseconomies in supply;
and the extent of areal benefit and cost spillovers.

The rising demand for urban government services

The share of local government expenditure in total spending
is increasing in almost all industrial economies. In the United
Kingdom, total local authority expenditure rose from 12·3
per cent of GNP in 1950 to 16·9 per cent in 1969, and the
rate of increase has recently been in excess of 9 per cent per
annum. Forecasts to 1981 and to 2000 prepared for the Maud
Commission indicated that local government services were
likely to claim an increasing share of GNP. There are many
reasons to justify this expectation: central government pressures on local authorities to develop their services combined
with a growing demand for higher standards; an expanding
population and, even more important, changes in its age structure favouring the old and very young who make heavy
demands on the social services; externalities and scale economies associated with increased urbanization make it more
efficient to supply some services in the public rather than the
private sector; social overhead investment required by an
extension of suburban development; the costliness of attempts
to solve the urban transport problem. Moreover, Baumol
(1967) has argued that most of the sectors comprising the
typical urban government service 'mix' are relatively techno-
logically unprogressive. This tends to raise costs cumulatively
because wage increases which spread from high productivity
sectors cannot be adequately offset by technical advances. He
concludes that

. . . inexorably and cumulatively, whether or not there is inflation, administrative mismanagement or malfeasance, municipal budgets will almost certainly continue to mount in the future, just as they have been doing in the past. This is a trend for which no man and no group should be blamed, for there is nothing that can be done to stop it.

Scale economies in local government

The actual average size of local government areas and the number of tiers in the administrative structure are usually the results of historical accident or a compromise between several often conflicting criteria. To search for a single optimal size of an urban government unit is utopian. The level of service at which costs are minimized varies from one service to another, and the public service 'mix' varies even among communities of the same size. Even if we could hypothesize a standardized city with a representative group of public services, the size of area which maximizes economies of scale may not be appropriate for administration or for raising revenue. Moreover, there are subjective non-quantifiable factors to be taken into account, such as the desire of citizens for personal participation in decision-making. This may favour small local government areas.

It might be easier to resolve these contradictions if the evidence on scale economies in the supply of public services was more conclusive. In fact, it is rather ambiguous. There are scale economies in some services, for example, water supply, local government administration, sewage plants, other main engineering services and probably public house-building, but not in the more important services. Studies in the United States, by Hirsch (1959) and Brazer (1959, 1962) for instance, are inconclusive. A critical problem is that the quality of service may vary with the size of the unit supplying it. Thus, *per capita* expenditure is likely to be a misleading indicator, and we need to devise measures which show the influence of scale on unit costs of homogeneous output (Gupta and Hutton, 1968). Another factor making it difficult to interpret what evidence is available is that motivation for productive efficiency in local government is weak: monopoly is the typical market structure; public goods either have no price or are priced in a manner which bears no relationship to production costs; the quality of service is often the result of a rigid matching of a fixed budget constraint to the population to be served rather than of a conscious desire to satisfy community preferences.[1] Moreover, as Isard (1956) demonstrated, we may be able to construct net economy curves for an individual service but these cannot be aggregated because of the weighting problem (the importance of a public service may exceed its share in total urban expenditures), and because of the interdependence of net economy curves.

Apart from scale economies, large units have certain advantages. They minimize areal spillovers in costs and benefits that can distort budget decisions. They usually have superior revenue-raising powers. Some public actions, such as measures to control air pollution, have to be undertaken on an area-wide basis or not at all. However, these facts do not establish an unequivocal case for large urban government areas since they have offsetting disadvantages. The possibility of diseconomies of scale and the loss of personal contacts and participation have already been mentioned. In addition, for certain services there is considerable spatial differentiation in the levels of benefit and such services are better supplied by small local government units. Finally, large units mean fewer units, and this restricts the choice facing mobile consumer-voters (see the discussion on the Tiebout hypothesis below).

To sum up, the size of area that enables services to be supplied most efficiently may not be a good size for financing, and the scale of area which permits maximum participation by the individual may be quite different again. If the optimal scale for each service varies, the ideal theoretical solution may be to have a separate area for supplying each service, but in practice the cumbersome nature of overlapping units, interdependence of investment decisions in different public services, and ad-

1. Admittedly, this is a difficult objective in the absence of an appropriate mechanism for aggregating individual preferences.

ministrative inconvenience would lead to inefficiencies. All we can say is that a multi-level system of government will be more efficient than a unitary structure.

The Tiebout hypothesis

A well-known analysis by Samuelson (1954) shows that there is no market solution to the determination of the level of expenditure on public goods. At the urban level, however, there is a quasi-market mechanism which may work, if imperfectly. Given that individual preferences differ and that social goods are paid for by a community's citizens, it is in the interest of individuals to associate with those with similar public goods preferences. An individual dissatisfied with his local expenditure-tax mix can register his preferences by moving to a more fiscally desirable community. The more numerous the communities and the greater their differences, the more likely that the consumer-voter will satisfy his preferences. Locational moves of this kind should lead to a more homogeneous set of preferences *within* each community, and this simplifies the task of determining the level and distribution of expenditures on public goods.

This possibility stems from a model by Tiebout (1956). However, there is not likely to be an optimal solution unless we make very restrictive assumptions: perfect mobility and knowledge, constant unit costs and no external economies in the supply of urban government services, and a very large number of communities. Moving from one community to another involves monetary costs. Individuals normally move only when changing jobs, and the choice of community is often restricted by area differences in job opportunities. Locational choice may be influenced more by factors other than the expenditure-tax mix. If costs vary with scale, a change in city population can result in variations in costs and output which in turn may induce dissatisfaction among consumer-voters; far from an optimal solution we may get continuous instability. External economies encourage fiscal integration, and large urban fiscal units make divergences between individual preferences and public services/tax structures more likely. Local public services may be financed in ways other than by taxes imposed on residents. For all these reasons, the gap between reality and the model is wide. It is thus often argued that the abstractions of the Tiebout hypothesis make it improbable that this quasi-market mechanism works.

Yet upon closer examination we cannot be sure that this conclusion is correct, particularly when intraurban moves are considered. Individuals working in the central city often have a wide choice of suburban communities in which to live, and the quality of services (such as local schools) or the level of rates (in the United States, property tax) may be of real importance in the choice of location. Tests by Netzer (1965) yielded unclear results, but a more recent study by Oates (1969) has given more support to the hypothesis. He carried out a cross-sectional analysis on fifty-three residential communities in New Jersey, within the New York metropolitan region. He used educational services to indicate the level of public services, and expenditure per pupil as a proxy variable for the output of educational services. The tests were based on the specific proposition that

If consumers, in their choice of locality of residence, do consider the available programme of public services, we would expect to find that, other things being equal (including tax rates), gross rents (actual or imputed) and therefore property values would be higher in a community the more attractive its package of public goods.

Since local property values were found to have a significant negative relationship to the effective tax rate and a significant positive correlation with expenditure per pupil, it appeared that people were willing to pay more to live in a community which provided a high quality level of public services (or in a community that gives the same programme of public services with lower tax rates).

Financing urban expenditures

The urban public sector is plagued with severe fiscal problems. Since urban government expenditures tend to rise faster than local revenues the resulting gaps probably require central government grants. Another difficulty is that there is often a spatial division between where a service is consumed and where taxes are levied, particularly due to the separation of homes from workplace. Taxable capacities and service requirements may diverge, especially in the central city, aggravated by the fact that existing fiscal systems fail to redistribute between the central city poor and the suburban rich. The large share of urban government spending in total investment (one quarter of the total in Great Britain) makes it necessary for the central government to retain some control over the aggregate level of spending and its distribution among major services. At the same time, it is desirable that urban governments have the widest discretion compatible with central control and should find ways of financing their own services wherever possible. The above problems can in most cases be eased by relying less on property taxes and rates and substituting non-property taxes, area-wide taxing and user charges. Practical and administrative obstacles in the way of raising revenue by these means may still require extensive dependence on central government financial support.

The three most common sources of finance are property taxes (rates), central government grants and user charges. Borrowing by local authorities may be an important source for financing capital spending programmes, but raises no problems which are different from those that occur in borrowing by companies or central government. Non-property taxes have their attraction as a local government financial source. A local income tax, for example, may more easily satisfy equity and ability-to-pay criteria. Local sales taxes are often appropriate for financing services provided for commuters. Experience with taxes of this kind is limited, however, and doubters lay great stress on the administrative difficulties. It is clear that if urban fiscal systems were being designed from scratch, taxes of this kind would have an important contribution.

From a theoretical viewpoint user charges offer the most satisfactory solution to the urban revenue problem. They represent the most obvious way of bringing payments more closely into line with benefits. They should tend to promote efficiency: firstly, by helping to balance demand with supply in cases (such as car parking) where excess demand leads to heavy social costs; secondly, by reducing misallocation due to services supplied to non-residents; and thirdly, by inducing higher standards of service. On the other hand, user charges are not feasible in many circumstances – because some urban services are indivisible, or because external economies and diseconomies arise, or because of the difficulties of measuring marginal social costs. Moreover, user charges may have adverse distributional effects that may make them difficult to introduce politically.[2]

Property taxes are by far the largest source of *local* revenue; rates in the United Kingdom account for 43 per cent of the financial resources available to local authorities, while the equivalent United States figure is 45 per cent. It is not easy to justify their use other than in terms of tradition and historical evolution. The usual rationalizations are that since the revenue raised is used to finance beneficial services benefits accrue to property as a result (e.g. police and fire protection), and that such a tax captures at least a part of the unearned increase in land values associated with increased urbanization. But most of the arguments are against property taxation rather than in its favour. If it predominates among local taxes, this means that taxes are imposed on some but not all forms of wealth. The tax rate varies for similar properties even within different parts of the same metropolitan region. The market value of a property has little relationship either to public outlays benefiting the property or to any expenditure costs incurred on its behalf. Property taxes are economically non-neutral in their effects: to the extent that investment in building is not price inelastic, they shift resources from investment in physical property to investment in human capital (probably beneficial since the social rate of return may well be higher on the latter);

2. The scope for user charges in urban government services has been examined by Vickrey (1963).

more seriously, they may reduce locational efficiency, especially within a multi-unit metropolitan area, if high rates divert new firms to less profitable locations; high rates on new central properties may discourage urban renewal, and so on. Netzer (1962) concluded that the property tax 'contributes to deviations from optimal land use patterns ranging from the severe to the ghastly'. Another drawback is that this form of taxation might divert too many resources into satisfying public wants. The reason for this is that although industry pays a relatively high proportion of property taxation it has little say in voting for higher taxes or for committing more resources to supplying urban services. It will pay consumer-voters to press for higher taxes since they will be the main beneficiaries of an increase in supply of services yet only have to bear a fraction of the cost.

Even if it is arguable that urban governments should finance their own expenditure programmes, the expenditure-revenue gap will probably also call for assistance by the central government. Grants from the central government can serve several purposes: to subsidize poorer urban areas; to stimulate expenditures on specific services; to help finance those local public services that confer external economies on non-residents or on the economy as a whole; or to ensure the attainment of minimum standards. Central government grants may be of several kinds: general cash (block) grants, unconditional specific grants or conditional specific grants. It is most unlikely that any single form of grant could fulfil the multiple policy objectives which influence the government to intervene in the supply of urban government services.

Considerable attention has been given recently, particularly the Heller–Pechman proposals in the United States (Perloff and Nathan, 1968), to the value of general cash grants. The case for these rests largely on the redistribution and fiscal imbalance arguments. Such grants need not necessarily interfere with resource allocation efficiency if by enabling poorer cities to improve their urban services they reduce the influence of differences in provision on migration decisions. Even more important, they provide a means of transferring rapidly growing central government revenues to urban governments faced with intractable fiscal problems. Baumol (1967) has emphasized the dilemma faced by the central city with the rapidly rising costs of its expenditure programmes and diminishing tax base. Since each city is in competition with others and with surrounding suburbs for industry and population, no city government acting alone can afford to increase its tax rates indefinitely. Another advantage of general grants, in this case probably a minor one, is that they economize on decision-making in conditions of indeterminacy. On the other hand, they are more costly to central government finances than conditional grants.

Specific grants are appropriate for stimulating merit want expenditures, for guaranteeing minimum standards of public services and for correcting for benefit spillovers by gearing grants to the ratio of spillouts to retained benefits. Specific grants may be unconditional or conditional. In the latter case, the conditions normally refer to matching requirements from local funds, though sometimes include controls over spending or restrictions on the type, quality and level of service. Conditional grants are less expensive than unconditional, but are more likely to distort free community choice by biasing spending in favour of grant-aided services.[3]

Implications of local government reform

Although the Maud Report (Redcliffe-Maud, 1969) is now unlikely to be implemented, it is nevertheless relevant to consider its recommendations on the provision and financing of local government services. It was argued that all personal services (education, welfare, health and housing) which are closely linked in operation and effect should be in the hands of one authority. Similarly, all services concerned with environment (planning, transport and major developments) should also be controlled by one authority. Furthermore, wherever possible the same authority should deal with both types of

3. Unconditional specific grants also have this effect though to a lesser degree (see Williams 1962).

service, since this would facilitate the optimal allocation of resources and enable community objectives to be served better. However, in some cases the appropriate area for planning contains too large a population to supply personal services (it is important with these services for elected representatives to keep in touch with the people affected) so that more than one authority is called for. There are other considerations to be taken into account. Many county boroughs are too small to command the resources and manpower to supply services efficiently, yet authorities must vary in size if areas are to match rationally the distribution of population. The Report recommended a minimum population of 250,000 for efficiency and a maximum of one million because of managerial diseconomies and the desire to preserve community participation potential. The application of these criteria led to a proposal for sixty-one new local government areas to be grouped, together with the GLC into eight provinces, each with its own provincial council.[4] In three metropolitan areas and in London it would be necessary to have two levels of authority, but the rest of England could be covered by unitary authorities.[5]

Another problem mentioned, though not in great detail, in the Maud Report is the need for new sources of local government revenue. It was argued that this was necessary in order to free local government from too much dependence on central funds (which finances about 55 per cent of local authority expenditure), while D. Senior stressed the importance of direct

4. The Commission for Scotland (Wheatley, 1969) also came out in favour of a two-tier system with thirty-seven district authorities at the 'shire' level and seven regional authorities. The regional authorities would deal with strategic and transportation planning, personal social services, fire and police, while the district authorities would be concerned with local planning, environmental and amenity functions, housing improvement and libraries.

5. In his minority report, D. Senior (Redcliffe–Maud 1969, vol. 2) argued for authorities based on 'natural' city regions defined in terms of service and community hinterlands, while accessibility and population size should determine the scale of authority supplying personal services. This implied a two-level structure, and Senior proposed thirty-five regional and 148 district authorities.

accountability: 'No system of local democracy can be viable unless its executive authorities are financially accountable to their own electorates'. Apart from miscellaneous trading revenues which contribute less than 10 per cent of local authority income, rates are the sole independent source of income. Suggested possibilities include local income tax, local sales taxes, petrol tax and motor licence fees. Local income taxation is now regarded as more practicable than formerly with the introduction of the corporation tax and the future computerization of Inland Revenue records. Local sales taxes which are fairly common in the United States[6] have been recommended by the Institute of Municipal Treasurers and Accountants. It would be a relatively simple operation to transfer motor taxation to local revenue. A balance needs to be struck between finding the local authorities a broader and income-elastic tax base and any fiscal complications resulting from assigning new taxing powers to them. Moreover, despite rising demands for urban government services, the aim is less to raise total taxation than to allow local authorities to obtain revenue directly, rather than have it raised by the central government and passed on to them in the form of grants.

6. In New York, for instance, there is a retail sales tax. This has two advantages. Retail establishments are less able to flee central city jurisdiction than manufacturing firms are, and there is some sense in concentrating on them. Secondly, to the extent that such a tax hits at consumers this is a reasonable attempt to make non-resident commuters pay for some of the services they undoubtedly enjoy.

7 The Urban Environment

Environmental problems are matters of increasing concern to planners and urban policy-makers. This concern takes the positive form of making urban life more aesthetically satisfying and pleasurable by means of attractive city centres, plentiful open spaces and recreational facilities, and good urban services and amenities. Its negative form consists of protecting environmental media such as air and water against the effects of pollutants and other waste residuals. Most recent research has focused on the latter.[1] Although many of the problems have yet to yield solutions, they must be given at least a passing mention. Of course, environmental questions arise in a much broader context than the city. Natural resource depletion, pollution of the ocean, pollution of one area's water supply by the actions of another area – these examples suggest that environmental problems crop up at the regional, national and international levels. But they are particularly prevalent in the city. In the first place, pollution generation rates are often a function of population size and density and hence are particularly high under conditions of spatial concentration. Secondly, there are marked similarities between environmental pollution and the more familiar forms of urban congestion such as traffic jams or strain on public service facilities.

Both phenomena are subject to large externalities. In all cases the problem arises when more than one agent is attempting to share a service or facility not provided individually for each user. The facilities in question – a road, the atmosphere, a river, a beach, a museum – are all public goods. In all cases,

1. See Ayres and Kneese (1969) and Rothenberg (1970). For a broader look at the problems of environmental quality see Perloff (1969).

the presence of other users can adversely affect the quality of services rendered to the individual. However, quality deterioration does not set in immediately, since each good has a capacity or threshold. Disturbance becomes noticeable only when capacity has been used up, but then it increases disproportionately. A further general characteristic is that action can be taken to increase capacity or to reduce the quality impairment: widening roads, installation of sewage treatment plants, recycling of waste residuals formerly effused directly into the atmosphere, rationing devices at swimming pools and museums, and so on.

On the other hand, although both phenomena can be treated as a form of social congestion – 'generic congestion' as Rothenberg (1970) calls it – there is a fundamental difference between them. With congestion, all consumers use the medium in much the same way and each is damaging the quality of service for others and himself to more or less the same extent. With pollution, on the other hand, some users abuse the medium (the polluters) while others are adversely affected by the pollution (the public); redistributional aspects of welfare become relevant. Rothenberg makes a distinction between pure congestion, where all users generate the same degree of congestion and share equally in the quality deterioration, and pure pollution, where some users generate very high rates of interference while others generate nothing but suffer from the quality deterioration. In the real world, most cases fall between these polar extremes: all users tend to generate impairment and share in its effects, but to different degrees.

Welfare theory tends to treat externalities as exceptional cases. Ayres and Kneese (1969) have argued that one class of externalities – the disposal of waste residuals – is a normal and inevitable part of the production and consumption process. Although goods and materials change form, the disposal of residuals involves, because of absorption of oxygen during production, a greater tonnage than basic materials processing (the latter is estimated at about 2500×10^6 tons per annum in the United States), though many residuals are gaseous and do not have to be handled physically. The economic implication of the generality of these externalities is that the partial equilibrium approach favoured by economists in dealing with technological external diseconomies is unsound theoretically.

The main contribution of the Ayres–Kneese study is to integrate analysis of residual flows, their recycling and their effects on 'common property' environmental resources into a Walrasian general equilibrium model of resource allocation. The tracing of the physical flows presents no difficulty but the pricing aspects are troublesome because of the public goods question. At least three items – the use of common property resources (air, streams, the ocean, etc.) as inputs, the use of environmental media in which to 'dispose of' wastes, and unwanted inputs (pollutants) in production – are transferred at a zero price, despite the fact that they may be scarce or may provide services or disservices. There is no market in which they might be exchanged. The solution in the general equilibrium model is to construct a surrogate market for them by using shadow prices. Thus, the common property resources are treated as a subset of raw materials, and are assigned shadow prices which represent, in effect, an income from the environment. These are treated as constants since, despite the use of shadow prices, their supply is not regulated by changes in relative market prices. The pollutants are introduced as a set of environmental disservices and are given negative shadow prices. The supply of these residuals can be adjusted by price changes, and this fact creates scope for imposing congestion charges on polluters. Although of conceptual importance, the general equilibrium model is not operational, since operationality would require specification of all preference and production functions including relations between residual discharge and external costs and of all possible factor and process substitutions. The partial equilibrium approach, despite its theoretical shortcomings, is convenient for policy measures to increase the assimilation capacity of media, or control the generation of pollutants.

Even so, it is difficult to treat one environmental nuisance in isolation. There are alternative forms that residuals from a given process may take. A community going to great lengths to protect water, for instance, is liable to pollute the atmosphere heavily, and vice versa. Or consider refuse disposal as an example: the main alternatives are incineration or dumping on landfill sites, but the former is likely to contribute to air pollution. The general point is that there is a high degree of interdependence among environmental quality programmes. A community wanting to protect all its main environmental media would need to invest heavily in recycling techniques for waste and to take action to promote low-polluting production methods. A similar point is that it is impossible to avoid the generation of some pollutants in a highly industrialized, densely populated economy no matter how much is invested to increase assimilative capacity. Thus, attempts to impose absolute standards are self-defeating. Instead, goals should relate to the achievement of tolerable standards. One difficulty here is that we have insufficient knowledge about the damage caused by pollution. Given limited budgets, it is important not to spend large sums of money on the elimination of harmless wastes while those that do a great deal of harm are generated unchecked.

As with other externalities, a general prescription to deal with pollution is to internalize the external costs. Some environmental problems are created over wide areas and cannot be dealt with by planners in one city. In this case, intervention by a regional or national government may be necessary to internalize the external costs, because the costs of pollution imposed on others may be external to the polluting city but internal to the region or nation. At the level of the individual firm or industry, taxes and congestion charges can internalize the external costs associated with particular pollutants by confronting managers with the social costs of their decisions and providing them with an incentive to organize their production in a different way. Responses might include technological changes in favour of lower waste-generating techniques, disposal of wastes on the site, that is by recycling, or locational shifts out of urban areas in cases where urban authorities levy exceptionally high charges on heavy polluting plants.

What determines the extent of a particular type of pollution generation or other kind of generic congestion? The main determinants are: the total output of the good generating the waste; the distribution of output among the polluter groups (who may have different generation rates per unit of output); and the capacity of the assimilative medium. In the economy as a whole, however, the total amount of waste residuals and pollutants generated is a function of the level of economic development (as measured by *per capita* income) and the rate of population growth. Growth and affluence *per se* will generate an increasing volume of congestion and environmental disturbance.[2]

The production of pollutants and other waste residuals is not a constant. The generation rate can be altered by investment, changes in materials processing technology, substitution of low waste-creating raw materials, and so forth. The investment to control pollution falls into two categories: *group treatment investment* and *social assimilation investment*. The former is undertaken by an individual polluter group and focuses on the particular externalities created by the group, for example smoke or fluid effluent from a particular industry. Polluters are unlikely to invest in this way unless they are faced with the social costs of their pollution, that is unless pollution or congestion charges are imposed. In this situation, the charges and group treatment investment become substitute outlays. Since there may be substantial scale economies in treatment investment facilities, investment of this kind will have greater appeal to large scale polluters.

Social assimilation investment usually takes the form of increasing the capacity of an environmental medium, and is

2. Since the growth in environmental control and policies is a product of increasing affluence, we have the ironic paradox that the forces inducing attempts to control deterioration in the environment are the very same forces responsible for that deterioration.

carried out collectively, that is by the government. It is, in part, a substitute for group treatment investment. However, since it is also a substitute for more production of the pollutant-generating good and all other goods in the economy, it needs to be justified in cost-benefit terms. This can be done in the usual way by comparing benefits with costs, where benefits are measured by the aggregate cost savings from reduced congestion minus the losses due to private treatment investment discouraged by the public investment, and costs are measured by the opportunity cost in terms of lost production of other goods and services. Since public investment of this kind is a positive function of the total environmental disturbance created by the population as a whole, it will be increasingly justified by population growth and income expansion. Growth may tend to favour a switch from private to public investment. Public investment does not require congestion charges to justify it. However, since some forms of congestion are better dealt with individually while others can be combatted more successfully collectively, there is usually scope for both private and public control. One difficulty with public investment for environmental control is that it may be impossible in practice to measure the benefits of reducing pollution, and in particular that 'intangibles' will be undervalued, leading to too low a rate of investment in environmental control. Consequently, it may be more sensible to express targets in physical terms. In this way, environmental goals relate either to standards of performance in attaining a prescribed reduction in pollution or to safety levels of pollution absorption. With goals of this kind, which are far simpler to handle than trying to assign monetary values to intangibles, the role of economic analysis is to show how these goals may be achieved most efficiently, for instance at minimum cost.

Apart from public investment decisions, the main policy choices in the environmental field are between prohibitive controls, *laissez faire*, and pricing methods. The first can be successful in some spheres, as shown by the relative success of the United Kingdom's Clean Air Act of 1956. In general, however, they are a blunt and inefficient instrument. Banning cars from city centres would help to guarantee a good environment, but the cost in allocative inefficiencies could be very great indeed. A do-nothing policy will also result in resource misallocation and is, in addition, increasingly unacceptable politically. The absence of congestion charges has several deleterious consequences. It means that goods subject to generic congestion are underpriced relative to other goods and too much is consumed. Similarly, within the industry in question heavy polluters produce too much in relation to light polluters. Environmental nuisances are not discouraged, and private firms will not find it worth while to invest in recycling or in new, less harmful, production techniques. Consequently, a great burden will be placed on the public sector to counteract the growing congestion and environmental problems.

In one special kind of environmental disruption, when consumers in general are both polluters and victims (for example the case of motor vehicle exhaust fumes), it is difficult at first sight to see why voluntary action will not be forthcoming. For instance, in the example quoted, the costs of an anti-pollution device on a motor vehicle are probably much lower than its potential benefits, so why are motor vehicle owners (as inhalers of fumes) not prepared to pay? The answer is found in the familiar phenomenon of neighbourhood effects. The individual's own incremental contribution to pollution control would be negligible compared with the aggregate contribution of the rest of the community. In this particular case, for instance, the benefits of anti-pollution devices on cars accrue from other people's devices, not from one's own, but the individual has to pay only for his own device while the costs of the devices from which he gains benefits fall on others. The individual without a device can profit from the fact that other people use them, and it will be in his self-interest not to install one. It can be shown, by using a variant of the n-person non-zero sum game sometimes called 'the prisoner's dilemma',[3] that if all individuals act like this, equilibrium is uniquely

3. For the details of the analysis see Reichardt (1970).

determined when all individuals fail to install the device. But the fact remains that society, and each individual, would be better off if everyone installed devices. With a very large number of individuals this can be brought only by a binding obligation, and this can be imposed only by the government either via compulsion or pricing methods.

The case for congestion charges is very strong. They provide scope for compensation principles to be applied to transfer income from the generators of social costs to the victims. Moreover, they provide some incentive for generators of pollutants to invest in treatment facilities that will reduce their tax liability. Most important of all, they increase allocative efficiency. The level of congestion charge should be such as to make the unit cost to the firm of generating an environmental disturbance equal to its marginal social cost imposed on the whole population. Less output of congesting goods will be produced, and external congestion costs will be lower. Moreover, the heaviest polluters will be the most heavily taxed.

The trouble with pollution charges is that they are difficult to impose in practice, since it is difficult to fix their level and incidence. Theoretically, the proper charge is that which makes the unit cost to the polluter of generating an environmental nuisance equal to its marginal social cost imposed on the community. But these marginal social costs may be impossible to measure, even approximately. In addition, there are severe technical obstacles and administrative problems involved in measuring the contribution of the individual polluter. This is necessary if we are to tax pollution generation itself not inputs or the final product, and we must do this if we are to improve allocative efficiency. It is arguable, however, that even if the appropriate theoretical pollution tax cannot be determined, the immediacy of environmental problems presents a case for justifying charges at that level which brings about a desired reduction in pollution generation and induces investment in recycling and abatement research. This pragmatism is strengthened if community environmental planning goals are concerned not so much with economic efficiency and resource allocation as with the satisfaction of human needs and improvement of the quality of life.

The above summary of some of the main environmental issues overemphasizes the negative considerations. It assumes that the natural environment is ideal and that man's interference with nature (the building of cities, for example) creates unwanted residuals and disservices. Its stress is on the effects of congestion on common property resources and on pollution control. In all these things, it is a good reflection of the content and direction of recent research.

On a quite different plane, environmental quality has a more positive side. The urban planner's role now becomes not the protection of nature against man's actions but improvement upon nature, the creation of urban beauty and aesthetic satisfaction. This is a difficult task which presents almost intractable problems. Beauty in urban design is a public good supplied without charge and not exhausted by its 'consumption'. This raises all the standard problems of pricing and incentives for the supply of public goods in a market economy. In particular, how do urban planners trade off quality with quantity? In the private sector, this raises no problem since consumers are usually offered a range of goods of different quality at different prices, and market decisions reveal the desired combination. In the public goods field, on the other hand, the decision to build, say, a new city centre can be a once-and-for-all decision and there is little opportunity for citizens to express their preferences. We know little about what constitutes a superior physical environment. Not only are we unable to measure beauty, but opinions on what is an aesthetically satisfying environment are subjective. Are the planners and design experts to be trusted, or should their schemes in any event be given extensive publicity in order to test public reactions? The trade-off between beauty and lower-cost utilitarianism is difficult to make, since urban policy-makers have enough trouble apportioning their budgets between competing urban investments, without taking quality differences into account. Accordingly, quality is very often determined residually, as a result of what can be afforded out of a given budget for a particular facility after the total urban budget has been divided. The best that can normally be achieved is that the facility, service or structure conforms to minimum performance and quality standards laid down in advance.

8 Economics and Planning

This book has been concerned with economic analysis and the problems of cities. Apart from passing comments on its effects, it has not treated the subject of planning extensively. To do so would broaden the scope of the book much wider than can be reasonably covered in a small text of this kind. It might also, since the boundary between planning principles and economic analysis is frequently blurred, lead to confusion about the separate contribution of economics to understanding the city. In any event, there are a great many planning texts available but few general books on urban economics.[1]

On the other hand, there are two aspects of the relationship between economics and planning that need to be discussed. First, we examine the 'pros and cons' of planning, with particular reference to how imperfections in the urban land market and other aspects of the urban economy make some degree of urban planning essential. Second, we consider as illustrations one or two economic (or quasi-economic) tools that have a wide application in planning.

Why planning?

The general case for government intervention in the allocation of economic resources rests on defects in market forces and the price mechanism. Urban planning falls within the scope of this general case. It is true, of course, that, in the past, some cities – particularly in periods of early and rapid industrialization – have grown up without any control, and have functioned

1. For general introductions to planning problems, readers may find Chapin (1965a), Goodman and Freund (1968) and McLoughlin (1969) useful.

reasonably well as economic units. What is unknown, however, is whether resources could have been allocated even more efficiently and, more important, how burdensome the social costs of unconstrained development were to successive generations of city dwellers. Almost certainly, market imperfections are greater in the city than in most other sectors and subdivisions of the national economy.

Many of these imperfections will be familiar to readers of earlier chapters in this book. Externalities are a general feature of the urban economy. Particularly important are spatial spillovers or neighbourhood effects, such as the disutilities to nearby activities of rundown property, environmental nuisances or the increase in welfare associated with proximity to a park or other urban amenity. Under the same heading we may include social congestion costs due to heavy traffic or aircraft noise. If individual uses of urban space are not forced to bear the social costs of their actions, maximization of individual profits cannot possibly lead to maximization of community benefits. Similarly, the failure to take account of external economies may mean that some socially beneficial investment decisions, extra-marginal according to private profitability criteria, will not be taken.

The market cannot easily cope with the problems created by the 'lumpiness' and interdependence of urban investment decisions. The provision of transport facilities is a clear example. It is true that in many countries railways, roads and canals were initially built by private companies. Yet this was made possible only because they did not get in each other's way, and because they shared out territory between them. Even in these circumstances difficulties arose because of lack of coordination at interchanges: gaps in the network, differences in gauge widths, and so on. The spatial concentration found in cities would turn such minor irritations into chaos if private enterprise attempted to deal with the urban transit problem. Another rather different point is that many types of urban facility are greedy consumers of land. Very often the ownership of urban land is fragmented and there might frequently be insuperable obstacles facing private enterprise's attempts to accumulate large parcels of land. The planner's weapon of compulsory purchase or eminent domain is the most clear-cut method of handling this problem.

Furthermore, we have noticed that many urban goods and services are public goods supplied at a zero price. There is normally no market for these goods, though, as pointed out in chapter 6, there is scope for adoption of user charges for some services, thereby creating a quasi-market. In these cases, however, the quasi-market is used merely to distribute the services not to produce them, so that the introduction of user charges usually assumes the prior existence of a public sector to supply the public goods. The acceptance of the need for intervention is not in itself the complete solution. Immense difficulties remain: how to specify the preference systems of individuals; how to resolve the unavoidable divergences of interest between private property owners and the general public when certain social goods (for example the provision of open spaces) are under consideration; how to marshal the resources necessary to provide the public goods required.

The urban land market does not work perfectly, but is characterized by rigidities and monopolistic elements. Local authorities and private owners frequently exercise monopoly power arising from the fact that some blocks of urban land have unique properties. There is a high degree of locational inertia because of high transfer costs, a desire to preserve invested capital in highly specific urban structures and a strong preference for avoiding the disruption of a change in location. At any point in time, a high proportion of urban land will be in sub-optimal use yet this land will not be brought on to the market. In particular, the urban plant in old central cities is often so out-dated that if private enterprise depreciation principles, such as are applied to industrial plant, were adopted, it would be scrapped. But, as Ullman (1962) has remarked, we cannot throw our old cities away. In these circumstances only the planners can save us. By compulsory purchase, by subsidizing redevelopment and by investing in improving the environment, planners may gradually bring about modernization of the urban fabric. The longevity and scale of urban investments imply that this inheritance from the past could not be handled by the market.

A more debatable 'deficiency' of the market is that it ignores the question of income distribution. The city brings the extremes of wealth and poverty together, and gives income inequality a spatial dimension particularly in the contrast between the central city and its transition zone and the wealthy suburb. Urban poverty is associated (let us make no pretence to discover a cause–effect relationship) with central blight, and it is probably ineffective to remove one without curing the other. If we accept Weimer and Hoyt's (1966, p. 13) dictum that 'urban economics deals with the effective use of urban resources in achieving community objectives', then it is clear that such objectives will include an income distribution component. It was argued in chapter 6 that urban governments should concentrate, from a fiscal point of view, on allocation problems and leave distribution and stability goals to the central government. But this is not always possible. Moreover, even if the central government assumes responsibility for income redistribution, urban governments and the planning mechanism may be among the instruments chosen for implementing this goal.

Many of the benefits of intervention by planners are implicit in the above imperfections in the market system. The economic justification for zoning and building controls, that is spatial spillovers, is a case in point. Without zoning, an individual could construct a building, say a factory, in the middle of a residential area in order to maximize his own profits, but these gains would be outweighed by losses (for example in property values) inflicted on neighbouring homes. If permitted, this location decision could be a destabilizing force leading to households moving out of the area (Tiebout, 1961). Moreover, if the private gains are more than offset by social costs, the community as a whole suffers a net loss in welfare. Zoning helps to reinforce the natural agglomeration forces of complementary activities and the repelling tendencies of incompatible activities. It also minimizes risks and uncertainty. Of course, an alternative to zoning is to make generators of adverse environmental effects pay the social costs they impose, by compensating the victims. Furthermore, where zoning restrictions are applied, these should not necessarily aim for strict separation of land uses. Some varied land uses are quite compatible and a judicious mix can save travel time and costs.

A wider aspect of externalities in the city does not depend on spatial proximity alone. It is arguable that in many modern cities external diseconomies predominate over external economies, so that continued expansion is inefficient and damaging to welfare. Yet this is not reflected in the costs and revenues of the individual firm. The firm gains from external economies created by others but does not take account of the costs it imposes on them. Accordingly, the individual enterprise may continue to expand its output even when increases in the city's output yield diminishing *social* returns. The alternative solutions to this problem are either to find ways of making private firms pay for their social costs or to impose direct controls on expansion. A practical difficulty with the former is that valuation of the social costs may be impossible because intangibles are often much more significant than measurable nuisance or congestion costs.

The planner exercises a number of functions that either cannot be carried out or are inefficiently performed by the market. The assembly of large tracts of land, particularly in central cities but also on the metropolitan fringe, and other resources necessary to provide urban infrastructure is one example. Resolving conflicts between competing groups and interests is another. Since most urban investment decisions hurt some interest or other, and in the absence of compulsory purchase and other controls minorities can often effectively prevent development, this arbitration by the planner may be crucial. Without it, backed up by the force of legislation, many urban investment and redevelopment schemes would never be undertaken at all.

If we argue that the main justification for planning is to correct defects in the market and the price mechanism, there is a danger of overemphasizing the negative aspects of planning. Urban planning is multidimensional, and is concerned with at least three frameworks: not only resource allocation (that is economic efficiency criteria), but goals and objectives (the pursuit of human needs and values), and design and forms (spatial arrangements). These frameworks are to some extent interrelated, and there are feedbacks from one to another. In this context, it is clear that there are non-economic considerations in community welfare, and of course these will be ignored by the market and the application of efficiency criteria. The planner cannot afford to ignore them. He may decide that the achievement of the community's goals necessitates deviation from the most efficient pattern of development. Even if this is the case, efficiency models remain useful. They can help in estimating the economic cost of deviating from the efficiency optimum, the costs and benefits of attaining alternative competing or complementary goals and they can show us how to use resources most efficiently given the goals. Planning should be goal-oriented, and it is this feature which gives urban planning its positive aspects.

Although the need for some degree of urban planning is more widely accepted than, say, the need for national economic planning, some people raise objections to it. To some extent these arguments conform to the standard case against government intervention. Why should planners make wiser decisions than private individuals? They may be wrong, and their actions would then reduce efficiency. Urban planning decisions are much more arbitrary than the guidelines of the price system. Even if planning can be justified in isolated instances because of deficiencies in the price mechanism, the net result of planning may be to hamper the operation of the price mechanism even in areas where it works well. These are familiar arguments. Of course, planning can have adverse effects. Since planning decisions are often on a greater scale than private market decisions and have wider repercussions on more people, a bad mistake by planners may be more harmful than a bad mistake by an individual firm. Moreover, individual errors, for example in forecasting, may tend to cancel each other out. But in the urban economy with a product mix inevitably containing public as well as private goods, both planning and the price mechanism have an allocative role. Similarly, there is no private institution capable of resolving the conflicts of interest that surround urban investment decisions. The antidote to bad planning is not no planning at all, but good planning.

There are more serious criticisms of urban planning, but these revolve around the question of the quality of planning rather than the bogus dilemma of whether or not planning is necessary in the first place. For instance, a common complaint is that planning controls may restrict the supply of land made available for development and that land shortage will force building to take place at locations and at densities that do not conform with what consumer preferences would have been in an unconstrained free market. But such an assertion may be either valid or invalid. One reason why planners may restrict the supply of building land may be to preserve open spaces or green belts. Using the land in this way may or may not be more in line with community preferences than using it for building.

Other criticisms are less equivocal. Planners may overemphasize structures and fixed locations at the expense of movement, communications and interaction. They may be preoccupied with the insular problems of an urban area enclosed by arbitrary political boundaries, neglecting the functional interconnections with settlements outside the boundary line (this constitutes a case for regional and area-wide planning, but that is another story). They may give too much attention to the city as a static system and ignore the importance of long-run change. Or, at the other extreme, they may evade subjecting their prescriptions to short-run efficiency tests by seeking the protection of the long-range future. Once again, however, these are not objections to planning *per se* but merely cautionary warnings to the planner. Sound planning can avoid these pitfalls.

Much more serious are the problems arising from goal-oriented planning. Planners and policy-makers have a wide variety of instruments (administrative, legal and physical controls, and financial measures), which are potentially available to attain their objectives. The trouble starts when planners attempt to clarify their goals. Goal formulation is probably the most critical aspect of urban planning, for if goals are correctly stated they can act as a standard against which even day-to-day decisions can be measured. Indeed, even the most trivial physical planning decisions cannot be justified unless the higher-order planning objectives have been specified. Yet this is not easy to achieve. The choice of goals is very wide. Some are economic (especially efficiency), others are not (quality of environment, density standards, open space requirements). Planning objectives may be in conflict, particularly when one of them is efficiency and others are social goals. Many goals are expressed in vague general terms, and need to be translated into measurable proxy goals for operational planning purposes. This is difficult because statistical indicators required to measure objectives are much sparser at the urban level than they are for the national economy. The existence of multiple goals creates taxing ranking and weighting problems.[2] Finally even if all these obstacles are overcome, there is still, despite the recent growth of interest in participation in planning, no mechanism for ensuring that the goals pursued by planners are consistent with the community's preference function.

Thresholds, cost-benefit and systems analysis

It may be useful to illustrate the potential links between economics and planning by looking at two or three tools, either borrowed from economists or analogous with techniques and concepts used in economics, which have been applied or sug-

2. See Richardson (1969a, ch. 14, 1969b, ch. 5) for analysis of these problems.

gested for planning. These are threshold analysis, developed by planners but using economic cost concepts, cost-benefit analysis, borrowed directly from economics, and systems analysis, an approach to problem-solving employed by economists in certain fields (pre-eminently military defence) but which is in effect interdisciplinary and also draws heavily on operations research and other quantitative techniques.

Threshold theory concentrates on the capital costs of urban development and stresses the importance of indivisibilities in urban investment projects.[3] These indivisibilities arise because as an urban area expands, it comes up against barriers – the 'thresholds' of urban development. These thresholds can be classified into three types: *physical* or topographical, for example where expansion requires building on, say, sloping land involving high construction costs; *quantitative* or technological, referring to capacity limitations in public utilities (sewage disposal, water supply, and so on); and *structural*, where expansion requires modification of the city's internal form particularly in the CBD. These thresholds are not absolute, but they are surmountable only by incurring high capital costs. In most cases the capital investment is required to accommodate an increase in population; thus urban expansion is measured by population increase not by growth rates in output nor is it expressed as a function of time. If threshold theory is valid, the growth of a city cannot be treated as a continuous process, but as a succession of jumps due to indivisibilities in urban investment requirements to accommodate growth in population.

Threshold analysis, the technique derived from threshold theory, aims at revealing certain categories of urban development costs associated with extension of the natural and man-made environment and showing how these costs might be reduced by planning. It is not a comprehensive planning

3. The technique was developed in Poland. For descriptions in English see Malisz (1969) and Hughes and Kozlowski (1967 and 1968). For criticisms and discussion see Lean (1969 and 1970), Famelis (1970) and Wright (1970).

technique but is most useful when planners are dealing with the problem of accommodating an exogenously determined specific increase in regional or sub-regional population, obtained, for example, as a forecast from an economic development plan. If the population is to be accommodated in one city the technique requires estimates of *per capita* threshold costs in different sectors of the city, in order to select the most efficient directions in which to expand. In some cases, further expansion may involve costs which are so high that the only feasible method of expansion is by decentralizing the new increments in population to satellite towns. If the population is to be spread over a number of settlements within the urban region the technique requires threshold-cost indices for each town. These will guide the planner to choose, unless other considerations predominate, the economically efficient pattern of development with the population increase optimally distributed from the point of view of urban development costs.

Threshold analysis has been subjected to a barrage of criticisms. Some argue that urban expansion is much more continuous than threshold theory suggests, for instance because there are many types of thresholds arising at different times, and because each time a threshold is crossed costs are for the moment reduced. Similarly, physical and structural thresholds are not as important in practice as in theory because activities can *gradually* adapt themselves to these limitations. This particular criticism is misdirected, since threshold analysis becomes particularly relevant only when a substantial increment of population has to be absorbed and planned for in a relatively short period of time. More serious is a related point: the fact that discussions of threshold analysis have concentrated on urban expansion as population increments, without paying much attention to the time period over which these increments are to be phased. Time is an absent dimension yet, since development costs are not constant over time and since even in the absence of inflation relative input prices change, when a particular threshold is crossed will affect the optimal development programme. This raises a doubt as to whether it is possible to draw up threshold cost estimates for towns and use them to plan an efficient pattern of development unless implementation is instantaneous.

A central feature of threshold analysis is that it emphasizes development costs and ignores both other costs (operating costs, social congestion costs, etc.) and the benefits of alternative patterns of urban expansion. Thus, some critics (Lean and Wright, 1970, for example) have compared the technique unfavourably with cost-benefit and cost-effectiveness analysis. If this means that it is a more limited technique, then of course the criticism stands. But it is difficult to avoid the conclusion that threshold analysis has been criticized for not doing something that it does not claim to do. It is very much a capital cost-minimizing technique and is really concerned with finding an efficient location pattern for allocating a planned or expected increase in population. It is not a substitute for a comprehensive planning evaluation taking into account benefits and anticipated revenues as well as all private and social costs. Cost-benefit analysis is, as observed below, most useful when we are concerned with the assessment of one single project or programme of projects or, at best, selecting from a limited set of alternatives. There are a great many possible combinations of distributing a given amount of urban population among a group of urban areas. The threshold technique is valuable as a preliminary to enable us to choose a limited set of 'efficient' distributions and to rule out patterns of urban expansion that are not feasible on development cost grounds (that is acting as a budget sieve).

Cost-benefit techniques have been widely applied by economists, particularly in the appraisal of public investment projects. They are being increasingly used in the urban planning field. If anything, the difficulties of the cost-benefit approach are magnified in this context. Plans are justified in terms of the whole community so that all costs and benefits, including many nonmeasurable items, have to be included. Most planning decisions benefit some interests but hurt others, so that the ratio of benefits to costs will vary from one group to another. Accordingly, it is difficult to avoid paying attention to equity as well as efficiency considerations. Moreover, many of the benefits fall within the public goods sphere and consequently have no market price as a guide to their value. For all these reasons, cost-benefit analysis must be handled with extreme care in urban planning. In particular, it would be dangerous to justify any planning project on the grounds of a single figure estimate of the maximized excess of the net present value of benefits over costs.

There are a great many pitfalls in the application of cost-benefit techniques: double-counting, the failure to list all benefits and costs, attempts to give spurious monetary values to intangibles, failure to adjust market price valuations to reflect imperfections in competition, choice of an inappropriate discount rate, the use of subjective ranking scales to order projects according to how far they are consistent with planning objectives. In addition, the technique is inapplicable in cases where the proposed project is so large that it will have an impact on the relative price structure. The cost-benefit technique must be used only as an aid to planning. It cannot take the planning decisions out of the hands of the planner, and it does not avoid the need to make value judgements.

Lichfield (1962, 1966 and 1970a) is one of the more cautious practitioners of the cost-benefit art in town planning. He describes his method as the 'Planning Balance Sheet'. This involves division of the community into several, assumed homogeneous, groups within the two broad categories of 'producers/operators' and 'consumers'. The costs and benefits are estimated separately for each group with the aid of 'instrumental objectives' which express the operational demands of each sector. The nature of these can perhaps be best illustrated by example: low financial costs, early development and scope for further growth for development agencies; amenities, location, choice and environment for consumers; safety, free flow of traffic and low accident rates for vehicle users; and so on. Costs and benefits are measured wherever possible. Measurable costs include land acquisition costs, capital costs for roads, services and construction, annual costs of vehicular travel, road maintenance, accidents, draining and public utilities, the gross annual value of lost agricultural output where agricultural land is absorbed into urban use. Measurable revenues accrue from commercial developments on the one hand and residential development on the other. Since the analysis is based on the costs and benefits for community sub-groups, some of the benefits gained by one group will be costs for another and neither for the community as a whole. These transfer items as opposed to real resource costs must be included in assessing the effects of a project on the individual group, but these positive and negative entries will cancel out in any overall estimate of community benefits and costs.

Many of the items in the planning balance sheet relate to non-measurable costs and benefits. These must be included to expose some of the implications of alternative proposals, and are the main reason why this method does not provide a clear-cut conclusion in terms of a rate of return or expected net profit from a particular project. The costs and benefits not measurable in money terms are either measured in physical or time units or where they cannot be quantified in any way are listed as intangibles. When several alternative schemes are under consideration (as in the Ipswich study, 1970) each scheme is ranked in terms of progress towards instrumental objectives. In the Ipswich study a simple ranking scale (numerical order of preference) was adopted, and the ranks were then summed algebraically to produce net totals for each sector and for producer/operator and consumer sectors as a whole. Of course, a ranking scale of this kind assumes a constant difference in value between each proposal and also equal weighting of sectors and instrumental objectives.[4] This could lead to the wrong conclusions, as Lichfield admits, unless one alternative shows up as the best in all circumstances. In the study quoted, there was sufficient unanimity to justify this crude ranking

4. Parry Lewis (1970) severely criticizes this approach, even though he strongly supports Lichfield's balance sheet approach in other respects.

scale. Had this not been the case, relative weights would have had to be assigned to the various sectors, objectives and differences between the alternative schemes, and a point-scoring system reflecting these would have introduced a strong element of subjectivity into the analysis. Another simplification particularly for comparisons between alternatives and/or between sectors is to reduce multiple entries by eliminating costs and benefits common to all, algebraic addition of entries, and capitalization of annual cost and benefit items or, alternatively, conversion of asset values to annual equivalents.

The planning balance sheet approach stops short of a standard cost-benefit calculus. Because of the wide array of intangible benefits accruing from urban planning decisions, the more modest objectives are welcome. The virtue of this approach is that it improves rationality in planning decisions by ensuring that all costs and benefits are enumerated and taken into account. It certainly does not avoid the need for value judgements. These arise in the selection of instrumental objectives, comparison of different intangibles between projects, choice of weights in entries and in the drawing of conclusions from the overall assessment of costs and benefits. In the Swanley study (Lichfield, 1966) one scheme involved markedly lower costs for producers and operators but also yielded lower net benefits to consumers, including benefit differences which could not be reduced to monetary values. In choosing between these schemes a value judgement could not be avoided. This places, of course, a heavy responsibility on the planners: making judgements on behalf of citizens, holding the balance between sections of the community with some objectives in conflict, and defending the interests of minorities and the next generation. The planner can hardly avoid these responsibilities in any event. Cost-benefit techniques give him a valuable aid in decision making; they do not relieve him of the burden of taking decisions.

Some weaknesses of cost-benefit analysis, such as the attempt to aggregate all benefits into a single benefit measure, are avoided by the looser, more generalized planning balance sheet approach. Nevertheless, a serious weakness remains, since the technique can be usefully applied only when the options have been restricted to a few clearly defined alternatives. This is all very well in cases when the planning objectives have been precisely specified and a development goal has been quantified and determined exogenously (for example when planners in a new town are asked to plan for the absorption of 50,000 overspill population from a metropolis). On the other hand, it is not a practicable way of dealing with the large number and great variety of planning problems with which planners have to contend.

Planning problems are characterized by their exceptional complexity. The urban planner has often to deal with several, often conflicting objectives, some of which are hard to quantify. Even if objectives can be agreed upon and ranked according to priority, there are frequently several alternative ways of achieving them. A compromise may have to be sought between cost minimization and technical efficiency, while each solution may have both advantages and disadvantages from the community's point of view. The range of options and possible courses of action are much wider than can be contained in a cost-benefit analysis.

What is required is a much broader approach to urban planning in which solutions are not pre-determined before the analysis, recognition is given to the impact of planning decisions on people, conflicts of interest are resolved, planning and administration are more closely integrated, information needs are foreseen and acted upon, allowance is made for the influence of the political process on decision-making, and the uncertainty of future outcomes in the long-run time horizon in which planners operate is accepted. Although this seems a very tall order, systems analysis[5] is a methodology potentially capable of meeting these requirements.

5. Systems analysis is a much overworked term. Its use here is not to be confused with its more familiar application – the design of improved systems for computer applications. Similarly, despite certain limited similarities such as the importance of goal identification, we are not

Systems analysis is a much broader version, because the determination of goals and objectives is considered as part of the problem rather than given, of cost-effectiveness studies but differs from these by relying on human judgement as much as on quantitative techniques and models. Quade (1964) has defined systems analysis as

... inquiry to aid a decision-maker choose a course of action by systematically investigating his proper objectives, comparing quantitatively where possible the costs, effectiveness, and risks associated with the alternative policies or strategies for achieving them, and formulating additional alternatives if those examined are found wanting. Systems analysis represents an approach to, or way of looking at, complex problems of choice under uncertainty ... In such problems, objectives are usually multiple, and possibly conflicting, and analysis designed to assist the decision-maker must necessarily involve a large element of judgement.

Thus, when defined broadly it refers to any analytical study designed to assist a decision-maker in identifying a preferred choice among possible alternatives. Sometimes (as in cost-effectiveness studies proper) attention is confined to a specific problem comparing alternative courses of action in terms of their costs and effectiveness in attaining some specific objective. For example, we might minimize the money costs of achieving a specified rate of intra-city traffic flow, or maximize the additions to the stock of city dwellings subject to a budget constraint. But emphasis on such narrow aspects of a problem is insufficient if the analyst is offering policy advice. He should also be concerned with: the specification of the right objectives, the determination of a satisfactory way to measure performance (criteria), the influence of non-monetary (social) costs, and the discovery of better alternatives. This higher-level approach, as opposed to the lower-level problems mentioned above, is the essence of systems analysis.

dealing here with the systems approach to urban planning urged by McLoughlin (1969). His emphasis is on the city as a system, in the sense of a set of interconnected parts which can be controlled by cybernetic planning techniques with their stress on monitoring and error-controlled regulation.

Systems analysis was developed during and after the Second World War in the United States for analysis of weapons systems, and many of its postwar applications have been in the defence field though in a wider context – general military strategy, deterrence, arms control and disarmament. More recently, it has been applied in the public sector generally, a process which culminated in 1965 with a directive to federal departments and agencies in the United States to install PPBS (programme planning and budgeting systems) involving, firstly defining long-range goals and objectives, secondly considering and evaluating alternative means of attaining objectives, thirdly analysing performance. As far as urban planning is concerned (with the possible exception of transportation planning), its application is still in its infancy, though there has been the occasional study in the United States, for instance that by Teitz (1968), indicating some of the more obvious problems. Planners are increasingly giving their attention to the complexities which cannot be resolved by reference to physical planning considerations alone, and which invite a systems approach. For instance, they are asking questions about how alternative arrangements would function, looking at the social costs of projects and acknowledging the existence of intangible gains and losses, searching for ways in decision-making to quantifiable elements, and taking account of the fact that planning decisions affect people.

The range of alternatives facing planners is so bewildering that it may be impossible for them to make a rational choice without the aid of systems analysis or similar higher level techniques. Yet these techniques are much more difficult to adopt in the urban planning field than in the analysis of military decisions (or, as in the case of operations research, in manufacturing and other spheres of managerial decision-making). There are a number of reasons for this. The precise specification of objectives is very difficult, and planning objectives have often to be stated in very wide terms. Operational criteria are difficult to adopt in the measure of effectiveness relative to costs, because the planner does not produce an 'output'. His success can frequently only be measured by performance measures and standards (persons per room and amenity standards in housing, for example) which are often expressed in input terms, and these make insufficient allowance for quality differences. Equity considerations have to be taken into account in urban planning decisions, and these are difficult to handle (as all welfare economists know). The constraints under which the planner operates may prevent him from considering alternative solutions to planning problems, and in particular he may have difficulty in freeing himself from the pursuit of narrow objectives (such as relating to design or structure). Most important of all, urban growth is the net outcome of a complex interaction between public and private decision-makers, and the long-run behaviour of the latter (that is households and firms) is very difficult to predict. This is particularly so because our models of urban development are so crude and elementary. To put it another way, systems analysis is most easily applied in cases where the organization itself controls the system, that is in closed systems (such as a nation's deployment of its military effort). But the urban economy is an open system influenced by important, independently determined exogenous forces, and this presents a severe complication.

References

ABRAMS, C. (1965), *The City is the Frontier*, Harper & Row.

ALONSO, W. (1960), 'A theory of the urban land market', *Papers and Proceedings of the Regional Science Association*, vol. 6, pp. 149–57.

ALONSO, W. (1964), *Location and Land Use*, Harvard University Press.

ALONSO, W. (1967), 'A reformulation of classical location theory and its relation to rent theory', *Papers and Proceedings of the Regional Science Association*, vol. 19, pp. 23–44.

ANDERSON, M. (1964), *The Federal Bulldozer: A Critical Analysis of Urban Renewal, 1949–62*, MIT Press.

AYRES, R. U., and KNEESE, A. V. (1969), 'Production, consumption and externalities', *American Economic Review*, vol. 59, pp. 282–97.

BAILEY, M. (1959), 'Note on the economics of residential zoning and urban renewal', *Land Economics*, vol. 35, pp. 288–92.

BAUMOL, W. J. (1963), 'Interactions of public and private decisions' in Schaller, H. G. (ed.), *Public Expenditure Decisions in the Urban Community*, Resources for the Future, Johns Hopkins Press, pp. 1–18.

BAUMOL, W. J. (1967), 'Macroeconomics of unbalanced growth: the anatomy of urban crisis', *American Economic Review*, vol. 57, pp. 415–26.

BECKMANN, M. J. (1968), *Location Theory*, Random House.

BEESLEY, M. E., and WALTERS, A. A. (1970), 'Some problems in the evaluation of urban road investments', *Applied Economics*, vol. 1, pp. 241–59.

BERRY, B. J. L., BARNUM, H. G., and TENNANT, R. J. (1962), 'Retail location and consumer behaviour', *Papers and Proceedings of the Regional Science Association*, vol. 9, pp. 65–102.

BERRY, B. J. L., SIMMONS, J. W., and TENNANT, R. J. (1963), 'Urban population densities: structure and change', *Geographical Review*, vol. 53, pp. 389–405.

BERRY, B. J. L., (1965), 'The retail component of the urban model', *Journal of the American Institute of Planners*, vol. 31, pp. 150–55.

BERRY, B. J. L. (1967), *Geography of Market Centres and Retail Distribution*, Prentice-Hall.

BLEICHER, H. (1892), *Statistiche Beschreibung der Stadt Frankfurt am Main und ihrer Bevölkerung*.

BLUMENFELD, H. (1954), 'The tidal wave of metropolitan expansion', *Journal of the American Institute of Planners*, vol. 20, pp. 3–14.

BLUMENFELD, H. (1955), 'The economic base of the metropolis', *Journal of the American Institute of Planners*, vol. 21, pp. 114–32.

BLUMENFELD, H. (1964), 'The urban pattern', *Annals of the American Academy of Political and Social Science*, vol. 352, pp. 74–83.

BOS, H. C. (1965), *Spatial Dispersion of Economic Activity*, North-Holland.

BOURNE, L. S., (1969), 'A spatial allocation-land use conversion model of urban growth', *Journal of Regional Science*, vol. 9, pp. 261–72.

BOVENTER, E. G. von (1969), 'Determinants of migration into German cities, 1956–61, 1961–66', *Papers and Proceedings of the Regional Science Association*, vol. 23, pp. 53–62.

BRAZER, H. E. (1959), *City Expenditures in the United States*, National Bureau of Economic Research.

BRAZER, H. E. (1962), 'Some fiscal implications of metropolitanism', in *Metropolitan Issues: Social, Governmental and Fiscal*.

BRIGHAM, E. F. (1964), *A Model of Residential Land Values*, RAND Corporation.

BRIGHAM, E. F. (1965), 'The determinants of residential land values', *Land Economics*, vol. 41, pp. 325–34.

BUCHANAN, C., *et al.* (1963), *Traffic in Towns*, HMSO.

CAMERON, G. C., and JOHNSON, K. M. (1969), 'Comprehensive urban renewal and industrial location – the Glasgow Case', in Orr, S. C., and Cullingworth, J. B. (eds.), *Urban and Regional Studies*, Allen & Unwin.

CAMPBELL, A. K., and BURKHEAD, J. (1968), 'Public policy for urban America', in Perloff, H. S., and Wingo, L., Jr (eds.), *Issues in Urban Economics*, Johns Hopkins Press, pp. 577–647.

CARROLL, J. D. (1955), 'Spatial interaction and the urban–metropolitan regional description', *Papers and Proceedings of the Regional Science Association*, vol. 1, pp. 1–14.

CHAMBERLIN, E. H. (1956), 8th ed., *Theory of Monopolistic Competition*, Harvard University Press.

CHAPIN, F. S., Jr (1965a), 2nd ed., *Urban Land Use Planning*, Illinois University Press.

CHAPIN, F. S., Jr (1965b), 'A model for simulating residential development', *Journal of American Institute of Planners*, vol. 31, pp. 120–25.

CHARLESWORTH, G. and PAISLEY, J. L. (1959), *The Work Assessment and Returns from Road Works*, Institution of Civil Engineers.

CLARK, C. (1951), 'Urban population densities', *Journal of the Royal Statistical Society*, vol. 114A, pp. 490–96.

CROFT, M. J. (1969), *Offices in a Regional Centre*, Location of Offices Bureau Research Report, no. 3.

CZAMANSKI, S. (1964), 'A model of urban growth', *Papers and Proceedings of the Regional Science Association*, vol. 13, pp. 177–200.

DARWENT, D. F. (1969), 'Growth poles and growth centres in regional planning: a review', *Environment and Planning*, vol. 1, pp. 5–31.

DAVIS, O. A., and WHINSTON, A. B. (1961), 'The economics of urban renewal', *Law and Contemporary Problems*, vol. 26, pp. 105–17.

DOHERTY, J. (1969), 'The distribution and concentration of immigrants in London', *Race Today*, vol. 1, pp. 227–31.

DONNELLY, T. G., CHAPIN, F. S., Jr, and WEISS, S. F. (1964), *A Probabilistic Model for Residential Growth*, Centre for Urban and Regional Planning, University of North Carolina.

DUNCAN, O. D. (1957), 'The measurement of population distribution', *Population Studies*, vol. 11, pp. 27–45.

DUNNING, J. H. (1969), 'The city of London: a case study in urban economics', *Town Planning Review*, vol. 40, pp. 207–32.

DYCKMAN, J. W. (1964), 'Planning and metropolitan systems', in M. M. Webber, *Explorations into Urban Structure*, Pennsylvania University Press, pp. 220–37.

ECHENIQUE, M. (1968), *Urban Systems: Towards an Explorative Model*, Cambridge School of Architecture, Land Use and Built Form Studies, W.P. 7

ECONOMIST INTELLIGENCE UNIT (1964), *A Survey of Factors Governing the Location of Offices in the London Area*.

ELLIS, R. H. (1967), 'Modelling of household location: a statistical approach', *Highway Research Record*, no. 207, pp. 42–51.

FAMELIS, N. (1970), 'On the validity of urban threshold theory: further comment', *Journal of the Town Planning Institute*, vol. 56, pp. 21–2.

GARRISON, W. *et. al.* (1959), *Studies of Highway Development and Geographic Change*, University of Washington Press.

GLAZER, N. (1965), 'The renewal of cities', in *Cities: A 'Scientific American' Book*, Penguin, pp. 186–202.

GOLDBERG, M. A. (1969), 'Intrametropolitan industrial location: some empirical findings', *Annals of Regional Science*, vol. 3, pp. 167–78.

GOLDBERG, M. A. (1970a), 'An economic model of intrametropolitan industrial location', *Journal of Regional Science*, vol. 10, pp. 75–9.

GOLDBERG, M. A. (1970b), 'Transportation, urban land values and rent: a synthesis', *Land Economics*, vol. 46, pp. 153–62.

GOODALL, B. (1970), 'Some effects of legislation on land values', *Regional Studies*, vol. 4, pp. 11–23.

GOODMAN, W. I., and FREUND, E. C. (1968) 4th ed., *Principles and Practice of Urban Planning*, International City Managers Association.

GREBLER, L. (1964), *Urban Renewal in European Countries: Its Emergence and Potentials*, Pennsylvania University Press.

GREEN, G. (1966), *Community Size and Agglomeration of Trade, Service and Other locally Orientated Industries*, Institute of Urban and Regional Studies, Washington University, St Louis, WP 5.

GREYTACK, D. (1966), 'Urban growth and import substitution in the service industries', Institute of Urban and Regional Studies, Washington University St. Louis, WP 7.

GUPTA, S. P., and HUTTON, J. P. (1968) *Economies of Scale in Local Government Services*, Royal Commission on Local Government in England, Research Studies, no. 3.

GUTTENBERG, A. Z. (1960), 'Urban structure and urban growth', *Journal of the American Institute of Planners*, vol. 26, pp. 104–10.

HADDON, R. (1970), 'A minority in the welfare state: West Indians in the London housing market', *New Atlantis*, vol. 2, pp. 80–133.

HAIG, R. M. (1926), 'Towards an understanding of the metropolis', *Quarterly Journal of Economics*, vol. 40, pp. 179–208.

HALL, P. (1969), 'Transportation', *Urban Studies*, vol. 6, pp. 408–35.

HANDLIN, O., and BURCHARD, J. (eds. 1963), *The Historian and the City*, MIT Press.

HANSEN, W. G. (1959), 'How accessibility shapes land use', *Journal of the American Institute of Planners*, vol. 25, pp. 73–6.

HARRIS, B. (ed.) (1965), 'Urban development models: new tools for planning', *Journal of the American Institute of Planners*, special issue, vol. 31, pp. 90–172.

HARRIS, B. (1968), 'Quantitative models of urban development: their role in metropolitan policy-making', in PERLOFF AND WINGO, pp. 363–410.

HARRIS, C. D., and ULLMANN, E. (1945), 'The nature of cities', *Annals of the American Academy of Political and Social Science*, vol. 242, pp. 7–17.

HEALY, K. T. (1965), 'Some major aspects of urban transport policy formation', in Universities – NBER Conference, *Transportation Economics*, Columbia University Press, pp. 327–45.

HERBERT, J. D., and STEVENS, B. H. (1960), 'A model for the distribution of residential activity in urban areas', *Journal of Regional Science*, vol. 2, pp. 21–36.

HERTZFELD, H. R. (1966), 'Physical characteristics of cities and regional growth', Institute of Urban and Regional Studies, Washington University St. Louis, WP 1.

HEWITT, J. (1964), 'The calculation of congestion taxes on roads', *Economica*, vol. 31, pp. 72–81.

HIGGS, R. (1969), 'The growth of cities in a Midwestern region, 1870–1900', *Journal of Regional Science*, vol. 9, pp. 369–75.

HILL, D. M. (1965), 'A growth allocation model for the Boston region', *Journal of the American Institute of Planners*, vol. 31, pp. 111–20.

HIRSCH, W. Z. (1959), 'Expenditure Implications of Metropolitan Growth and Consolidation', *Review of Economics and Statistics*, vol. 41, pp. 232–41.

HOOVER, E. M. (1968), 'The evolving form and organization of the metropolis', in PERLOFF AND WINGO, pp. 237–83.

HOYT, H. (1939), *The Structure and Growth of Residential Neighbourhoods in American Cities*, Chicago University Press.

HUFF, D. L. (1961), 'Ecological characteristics of consumer behaviour', *Papers and Proceedings of the Regional Science Association*, vol. 7, pp. 19–28.

HUFF, D. L. (1966), *Determination of Intra-Urban Retail Trade Areas*, Graduate School of Business Administration, University of California, Los Angeles.

HUGHES, J. T., and KOZLOWSKI, J. (1967), 'Urban threshold theory and analysis', *Journal of the Town Planning Institute*, vol. 53, pp. 55–60.

HUGHES, J. T., and KOZLOWSKI, J. (1968), 'Threshold analysis – an economic tool for town and regional planning', *Urban Studies*, vol. 5, pp. 132–43.

HURD, R. M. (1903), *Principles of City Land Values*, The Record and Guide, New York.

IKLÉ, F. C. (1954), 'Sociological relationship of traffic to population and distance', *Traffic Quarterly*, vol. 8.

ISARD, W. (1956), *Location and Space-Economy*, MIT Press.

JACOBS, J. (1961), *The Death and Life of Great American Cities*, Random House.

JOHNSON M. B. (1964), 'On the economics of road congestion', *Econometrica*, vol. 32, pp. 137–150.

JONES, C. S. (1969), *Regional Shopping Centres: Their Location, Planning and Design*, Business Books.

KAIN, J. F. (1962), 'The journey-to-work as a determinant of residential location', *Papers and Proceedings of the Regional Science Association*, vol. 9, pp. 137–60.

KAIN, J. F. (1969), 'A reappraisal of metropolitan transport planning', paper read at Seminar for Urban and Regional Research, University of Washington.

KNOS, D. S. (1962), *Distribution of Land Values in Topeka, Kansas*, Centre for Research in Business, University of Kansas.

KUENNE, R. E. (1963), *The Theory of General Economic Equilibrium*, Princeton University Press.

KUHN, T. E. (1965), 'The economics of transportation planning in urban area', in Universities – NBER Conference, *Transportation Economics*, Columbia University Press, pp. 297–321.

KUZNETS, S. (1964), *Population Redistribution and Economic Growth, United States, 1870–1950: III. Demographic Analysis and Interrelations*, The American Philosophical Society, Philadelphia.

LAKSHMANAN, T. R., and HANSEN, W. G. (1965), 'A retail market-potential model', *Journal of the American Institute of Planners*, vol. 31, pp. 134–43.

LAMPARD, E. E. (1954–5), 'The history of cities in economically advanced areas', *Economic Development and Cultural Change*, vol. 3, pp. 81–136.

LAMPARD, E. E. (1963), 'Urbanization and social change: on broadening the scope and relevance of urban history', in HANDLIN AND BURCHARD, pp. 225–47.

LANSING, J. B. (1966), *Residential Location and Urban Mobility; The Second Wave of Interviews*, Survey Research Centre, Michigan.

LANSING, J. B., and MUELLER, E. (1964), *Residential Location and Urban Mobility*, Survey Research Centre, Michigan.

LAPIN, H. S. (1964), *Structuring the Journey to Work*, Pennsylvania University Press.

LATHROP, G. T., and HAMBURG, J. R. (1965), 'An opportunity-accessibility model for allocating regional growth', *Journal of the American Institute of Planners*, vol. 31, pp. 95–103.

LAURENTI, L. (1960), *Property Values and Race*, California University Press.

LEAN, W. (1969), 'An economist's note on the validity of urban threshold theory', *Journal of the Town Planning Institute*, vol. 55 p. 311.

LEAN, W. (1970), 'On the validity of urban threshold theory: a rejoinder', *Journal of the Town Planning Institute*, vol. 56, pp. 106–7.

LICHFIELD, N. (1962), *Cost-Benefit Analysis in Urban Redevelopment*, University of California Real Estate Research Program, Berkeley, Research Report no. 20.

LICHFIELD, N. (1966), 'Cost-benefit analysis in town planning: a case study, Swanley', *Urban Studies*, vol. 3, pp. 215–49.

LICHFIELD, N., and CHAPMAN, H. (1970a), 'Cost benefit analysis in urban expansion: a case study, Ipswich', *Urban Studies*, vol. 7, pp. 153–88.

LICHFIELD, N., *et al* (1970b), *Stevenage Public Transport – Cost–Benefit Analysis*, Stevenage Development Corporation.

LIEBERSON, S. (1963), *Ethnic Patterns in American Cities*, Free Press.

LINDHOLM, R. W. (ed.) (1967), *Property Taxation USA*, Wisconsin University Press.

LITTLE, ARTHUR D., INC. (1966a), *Model of San Franciscan Housing Market*, San Francisco Community Renewal Program, Technical Paper no. 8.

LITTLE, ARTHUR D., INC. (1966b), *Community Renewal Programming*, Praeger.

LOCATION OF OFFICES BUREAU (1970), *Annal Report*, 1969–70.

LOEWENSTEIN, L. K. (1965), *The Location of Residences and Workplaces in Urban Areas*, Scarecrow Press.

LOWRY, I. S. (1964), *A Model of Metropolis*, RAND Corporation.

LOWRY, I. S. (1966), *Migration and Metropolitan Growth: Two Analytical Models*, Chandler Publishing Co.

LOWRY, I. S. (1967), *Seven Models of Urban Development: A Structural Comparison*, RAND Corporation.

MALISZ, B. (1969), 'Implications of threshold theory for urban and regional planning', *Journal of Town Planning Institute*, vol. 55, pp. 108–10.

MARCUS, M. (1965), 'Agglomeration economics: a suggested approach' *Land Economics*, vol. 41, pp. 279–84.

MCAUSLAN, J, (1966), 'Residential land values, 1962–65', *The Chartered Surveyor*, vol. 213, pp. 598–609.

MCLOUGHLIN, J. B. (1969), *Urban and Regional Planning: A Systems Approach*, Faber.

MEDHURST, F., and PARRY LEWIS, J. (1969), *Urban Decay: An Analysis and a Policy*, Macmillan.

MEIER, R. L. (1963), 'The organization of technological innovation in urban environments', in HANDLIN AND BURCHARD pp. 74–83.

MEYER, J. R., KAIN, J. F., and WOHL, M. (1965), *The Urban Transportation Problem*, Harvard University Press.

MILLS, E. S. (1967), 'An aggregative model of resource allocation in a metropolitan area', *American Economic Review*, vol. 57, pp. 197–210.

MILLS, E. S. (1969), 'The value of land', in H. S. Perloff (ed.), *The Quality of the Urban Environment*, Johns Hopkins Press, pp. 231–53

MINISTRY OF TRANSPORT (SMEED PANEL) (1964), *Road Pricing: The Economic and Technical Possibilities*, HMSO.

MITCHELL, R. B., and RAPKIN, C. (1954), *Urban Traffic: A Function of Land Use*, Columbia University Press.

MORRILL, R. L. (1965), *Migration and the Spread and Growth of Urban Settlements*, Lund Studies in Geography, series B, Human Geography, no. 26.

MOSES, L. N. (1962), 'Towards a theory of intra-urban wage differentials and their influence on travel patterns', *Papers and Proceedings of the Regional Science Association*, vol. 9, pp. 53–63.

MOSES, L. N. and WILLIAMSON, H. F., Jr. (1963), 'Value of time, choice of mode, and the subsidy issue in urban transportation', *Journal of Political Economy*, vol. 71, pp. 247–64.

MOSES, L. N., and WILLIAMSON, H. F., Jr. (1967), 'The location of economic activities in cities', *American Economic Review*, vol. 57, pp. 211–21.

MUELLER, M. G. (1966), *Readings in Macroeconomics*, Holt, Rinehart & Winston.

MUSGRAVE, R. A. (1969), 'Theories of fiscal federalism', *Public Finance*, vol. 24, pp. 521–32.

MUTH, R. F. (1961), 'The spatial structure of the housing market', *Papers and Proceedings of the Regional Science Association*, vol. 7, pp. 207–20.

MUTH, R. F. (1968a), 'Urban residential land and housing markets', in Perloff and Wingo, pp. 285–330.

MUTH, R. F. (1968b), 'Differential growth among large US cities', Institute for Urban and Regional Studies, Washington University, St Louis, WP 15.

MUTH, R. F. (1969), *Cities and Housing*, Chicago University Press.

NATIONAL BUILDING AGENCY (1968), *Land Costs and Housing Development*.

NEEDLEMAN, L. (1965), *The Economics of Housing*, Staples Press.

NEEDLEMAN, L. (1968), 'Rebuilding or renovation: reply', *Urban Studies*, vol. 5, pp. 86–90.

NEEDLEMAN, L. (1969), 'The comparative economics of improvement and new building, Urban Studies, vol. 6, pp. 196–209.

NETZER, D. (1962), 'The property tax and alternatives in urban development', *Papers and Proceedings of the Regional Science Association*, vol. 9, pp. 191–200.

NETZER, D. (1965), *Economics of the Property Tax*, Brookings Institution.

NETZER, D. (1968), 'Federal, state and local finance in a metropolitan context', in PERLOFF AND WINGO, pp. 435–74.

NETZER, D. (1970), *Economics and Urban Problems: Diagnoses and Prescriptions*, Basic Books.

NEUTZE, G. M. (1969), 'The price of land for urban development', seminar paper, Urban Research Unit, Australian National University, Canberra.

OATES, W. E. (1969), 'The effects of property taxes and local spending on property values: an empirical study of tax capitalization and the Tiebout hypothesis', *Journal of Political Economy*, vol. 77, pp. 957–71.

OI, W., and SHULDINER, P. (1962), *An Analysis of Urban Travel Demands*, Northwestern University Press.

OWEN, W. (1966), *The Metropolitan Transport Problem*, Brookings Institution.

PARRY LEWIS, J. (1970), 'The invasion of planning', *Journal of the Town Planning Institute*, vol. 56, pp. 100–103.

PEGRUM, F. D. (1963), *Urban Transport and the Location of Industry in Metropolitan Los Angeles*, Bureau of Business and Economic Research, Los Angeles.

PERLOFF, H. S. (ed.) 1969, *Quality of the Urban Environment*, Johns Hopkins Press.

PERLOFF, H. S., DUNN, E. S., Jr., LAMPARD, E. E., and MUTH, R. F. (1960), *Regions, Resources and Economic Growth*, Johns Hopkins Press.

PERLOFF, H. S., and NATHAN, R. P. (eds.) (1968), *Revenue Sharing and the City*, Johns Hopkins Press.

PERLOFF, H. S. and WINGO, L. Jr. (eds.) (1968), *Issues in Urban Economics*, Johns Hopkins Press.

PFOUTS, R. W. (1958), 'Reply to Harris on testing – the Base Theory', *Journal of American Institute of Planners*, vol. 24, pp. 238–43.

PRED, A. R. (1966), *The Spatial Dynamics of U.S. Urban-Industrial Growth, 1800–1914*, MIT Press.

PREST, A. R., and TURVEY, R. (1965), 'Cost–benefit analysis: a survey', *Economic Journal*, vol. 75, pp. 683–735.

PRESTON, R. E. (1966), 'The zone in transition: a study of urban land use patterns', *Economic Geography*, vol. 42, pp. 236–59.

QUADE, E. S. (ed.) (1964), *Analysis for Military Decisions*, North Holland.

QUARMBY, D. A. (1967), 'Travel mode for journey to work', *Journal of Transport Economics and Policy*, vol. 1, pp. 297–300.

REDCLIFFE-MAUD, LORD (1969), *Royal Commission on Local Government in England*, 3 vols, (Cmnd. 4040), HMSO.

REICHARDT, R. (1970), 'Dilemmas of economic behaviour *vis-à-vis* environmental pollution', *Kyklos*, vol. 23, pp. 849–65.

REYNOLDS, D. J. (1966), *Economics, Town Planning and Traffic*, Institute of Economic Affairs.

RICHARDSON, H. W. (1969a), *Regional Economics: Location Theory, Urban Structure and Regional Change*, Weidenfeld and Nicolson.

RICHARDSON, H. W. (1969b), *Elements of Regional Economics*, Penguin.

ROTH, G. J. (1966), *Paying for Parking*, Hobart Paper no. 33, Institute of Economic Affairs.

ROTHENBERG, J. (1967), *Economic Evaluation of Urban Renewal: Conceptual Foundations of Benefit–Cost Analysis*, Brookings Institution.

ROTHENBERG, J. (1970), 'The economics of congestion and pollution: an integrated view', *American Economic Review*, vol. 60, Papers, pp. 114–21.

ROW, A., and JURKAT, E. (1959), 'The economic forces shaping land use patterns', *Journal of the American Institute of Planners*, vol. 25, pp. 77–81.

SAMUELSON, P. A. (1954), 'The pure theory of public expenditures', *Review of Economics and Statistics*, vol. 36, pp. 387–9.

SCHLAGER, K. J. (1965), 'A land use plan design model', *Journal of the American Institute of Planners*, vol. 31, pp. 103–11.

SCHNORE, L. F. (1957), 'Metropolitan growth and decentralization', *American Journal of Sociology*, vol. 63, pp. 171–80.

SCHNORE, L. F. (1962), 'The use of public transportation in urban areas', *Traffic Quarterly*, vol. 16, pp. 488–98.

SCHNORE, L. F. (1965), *The Urban Scene*, Free Press.

SHARP, C. (1966), 'Congestion and welfare – an examination of the case for a congestion tax', *Economic Journal*, vol. 76, pp. 806–17.

SIGSWORTH, E. M., and WILKINSON, R. K. (1967), 'Rebuilding or renovation?', *Urban Studies*, vol. 4, pp. 109–21.

SMEED, R. J. (1961), 'The traffic problem in towns', paper read at the Manchester Statistical Society.

SMITH, W. F. (1969), 'Optimum lot size when site rent is a transfer payment', *Annals of Regional Science*, vol. 3, pp. 8–15.

SOLOMON, E., and BILBIJA, Z. G. (1959), *Metropolitan Chicago: An Economic Analysis*, Free Press.

SOUTH EAST JOINT PLANNING STUDY (1971), *The Location of Industry*, Research Studies, vol. 1.

STEGER, W. A. (1965), 'The Pittsburgh urban renewal simulation model', *Journal of American Institute of Planners*, vol. 31, pp. 144–50.

STEGMAN, M. A. (1969), 'Accessibility models and residential location', *Journal of American Institute of Planners*, vol. 35, pp. 22–9.

STEVENS, B. H., and BRACKETT, C. A. (1967), *Industrial Location*, Bibliography Series, no. 3, Regional Science Research Institute.

STILWELL, F. J. B. (1969), 'Regional growth and structural adaptation', *Urban Studies*, vol. 6, pp. 162–78.

SWERDLOFF, C. N., and STOWERS, J. R. (1966), 'A test of some first generation residential land use models', *Highways Research Record*, no. 126.

TAEUBER, K. E. and TAEUBER, A. F. (1965), *Negroes in Cities: Residential Segregation and Neighbourhood Changes*, Aldine.

TEITZ, M. B. (1968), 'Cost effectiveness: a systems approach to analysis of urban services', *Journal of the American Institute of Planners*, vol. 34, pp. 303–11.

THOMPSON, W. R. (1965), *A Preface to Urban Economics*, Johns Hopkins Press.

TIEBOUT, C. M. (1956), 'A pure theory of local expenditures', *Journal of Political Economy*, vol. 64, pp. 416–24.

TIEBOUT, C. M. (1961), 'Intra-urban location problems: an evaluation', *American Economic Review*, vol. 51, Papers, pp. 271–8.

TINBERGEN, J. (1961) 'The spatial dispersion of production: a hypothesis', *Schweizerishe Zeitschrift für Volkwirtschaft und Statistik*, vol. 97, pp. 412–19.

TOWNROE, P. M. (1970), 'Industrial linkage, agglomeration and external economies', *Journal of Town Planning Institute*, vol. 56, pp. 18–20.

TSURU, S. (1963), 'The economic significance of cities', in HANDLIN AND BURCHARD, pp. 44–55.

TURVEY, R. (1957), *The Economics of Real Property*, Allen & Unwin.

ULLMAN, E. (1958), 'Regional development and the geography of concentration', *Papers and Proceedings of the Regional Science Association*, vol. 4, pp. 179–88.

ULLMAN, E. (1968), 'The nature of cities reconsidered', *Papers and Proceedings of the Regional Science Association*, vol. 9. pp. 7–23.

VANCE, J. E., Jr. (1964), *Geography and Urban Evolution in the San Francisco Bay area*, Berkeley University Press.

VERNON, R. (1960), *Metropolis 1985*, Harvard University Press.

VICKREY, W. S. (1963), 'General and specific financing of urban services', in Schaller, H. G. (ed.), *Public Expenditure Decisions in the Urban Community*, Johns Hopkins Press, pp. 62–90.

VICKREY, W. S. (1965), 'Pricing as a tool in coordination of local transportation' in universities – NBER Conference, *Transportation Economics*, Columbia University Press, pp. 275–91.

VOORHEES, A. (1968), 'Land use transportation studies', *Journal of the Town Planning Institute*, vol. 54, pp. 331–7.

WABE, J. S. (1966), 'Office decentralization: an empirical study', *Urban Studies*, vol. 3, pp. 35–55.

WALTERS, A. A. (1961), 'The theory and measurement of private and social cost of highway congestion', *Econometrica*, vol. 29, pp. 676–99.

WEBBER, M. M. (1964), 'The urban place and the nonplace urban realm', in Webber, M. M., *et. al.*, *Explorations into Urban Structure*, Pennsylvania University Press, pp. 79–153.

WEIMER, A. M., and HOYT, H. (1966), *Principles of Real Estate*, Ronald Press, 5th ed.

WEISS, S. J. AND GOODING, E. C. (1968), 'Estimation of differential multipliers in a small regional economy', *Land Economics*, vol. 44, pp. 235–44.

WENDT, P. F. (1957), 'Theory of urban land values', *Land Economics*, vol. 33, pp. 228–40.

WHEATLEY, LORD (1969), *Royal Commission on Local Government in Scotland*, (Cmnd. 4150), HMSO.

WILLIAMS, A. (1962), *Public Finance and Budgetary Policy*, Allen & Unwin.

WILLIAMSON, J. G., and SWANSON, J. A. (1966), 'The growth of cities in the American Northeast, 1820–70', *Explorations in Entrepreneurial History*, vol. 4., supplement, pp. 3–101.

WILSON, A. G., (1968), 'Development of some elementary residential location models', Centre for Environmental Studies, WP 22.

WINGER, A. R. (1969), 'Supply oriented urban economic models', *Journal of American Institute of Planners*, vol. 35, pp. 30–4.

WINGO, L. Jr (1961), *Transportation and Urban Land*, Johns Hopkins Press.

WINGO, L. Jr (1966), 'Urban renewal strategy for information analysis', *Journal of American Institute of Planners*, vol. 32, pp. 143–54.

WINGO, L. Jr, and PERLOFF, H. S. (1961), 'The Washington transportation plan: technics or politics?', *Papers and Proceedings of the Regional Science Association*, vol. 7, pp. 49–62.

WRIGHT, W. D. C. (1970), 'A comparison between cost-effectiveness and threshold analysis', *Journal of Town Planning Institute*, vol. 56, p. 149.

YEATES, M. (1965), 'Some factors affecting the spatial distribution of Chicago land values', *Economic Geography*, vol. 41, pp. 57–70.

Index